The
Korean
Book of
Happiness

Author Note: In this book, the word Korea refers to South Korea.

First published in Great Britain in 2023 by Short Books, an imprint of
Octopus Publishing Group Ltd
Carmelite House
50 Victoria Embankment
London EC4Y 0DZ
www.octopusbooks.co.uk

An Hachette UK Company
www.hachette.co.uk

ISBN 978-1-78072-575-8

A CIP catalogue record for this book is available from the British Library.

Printed and bound in the United Kingdom

10 9 8 7 6 5 4 3 2 1

This FSC® label means that materials used for the product have been
responsibly sourced

MIX
Paper from
responsible sources
FSC® C104740

The Korean Book of Happiness

Joy, Resilience and the Art of Giving

Barbara
J. Zitwer

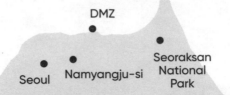

DMZ

Seoul Namyangju-si

Seoraksan
National
Park

South
Korea
대한민국

Taebaeck
Mountains

Unmunsa
Monastery

Busan

Jindo
Island

Jeju
Island

*This book is dedicated to all the Korean writers I represent
who so generously shared their books and their country with me.
And to all the skilled translators who make it possible for us
to read these amazing works.*

Table of Contents

Introduction:
Welcome to Korea

한국에 오신 것을 환영합니다

Hangoogeh ohshin geuseol hwanyounghapnidah

I stepped into Korea by a quirk of fate.

Twenty-two years ago, I set up my own literary agency in New York. I built up the business and my reputation off the back of my ability to discover new authors. But after twelve years, I was struggling to find writers that I could get truly passionate about – passion and love are the only things that drive me.

That spring, I met my Korean co-agent Joseph Lee for the first time when he came to visit New York. We had dinner together and I found him to be a charming, warm man with a great understanding of Western literature.

At an Italian restaurant, over pasta and red wine, I suddenly blurted out, "Don't you have any hot, new young writers I can represent?"

At first, he looked quizzical, and then he smiled. "Yes, many!" he answered.

It turned out no one had asked him that question before. He had spent years selling international books into Korea, but never Korean books to the world.

He told me about a young author named Young-ha Kim and his book, *I Have The Right to Destroy Myself.* The title grabbed me instantly. He immediately called the author and within minutes I was speaking to him. His was the first Korean book I sold, and the beginning of it all.

In 2009, when twenty pages of an English translation of Korean author Kyung-sook Shin's *Please Look After Mom* landed on my desk, I saw its enormous potential.

Her ground-breaking novel about a neglected mother was like nothing I had ever read, an overwhelmingly emotional, yet unsentimental mother's story told from the points of view of her children and husband. The discovery was enthralling.

For me, Kyung-sook's novel was also a rabbit hole into more Korean literature – and I happily dived in. I was particularly entranced with books authored by female writers, whose stories were original expressions of the repression, isolation and alienation of women. Here were books I desperately wanted to represent – yet there was resistance at first.

"What's with you and all those Korean books no one has ever heard of?" publishers and editors constantly wondered. They had never encountered Korean literature and thought I was a bit nutty. Most people thought of Korea as North Korea, with its atomic bomb threats and mad totalitarian dictator sporting a shiny, black pudding-bowl haircut and a big belly.

But Kyung-sook's book turned out to be the starter pistol. *Please Look After Mom* went on to become a *New York Times* bestseller, convincing publishers around the globe that readers were ready and hungry for Korean writers. (It has sold into 35 countries and in 2011, it won the Man Asian Prize).

I had found a cause, not just a job. I became obsessed with helping Korean authors get published around the world, and I am proud to say I succeeded.

My client Hang Kang won the 2014 Booker Translation Prize for *The Vegetarian*. Yun Ko-eun was the first Korean to win the CWA Dagger Prize for Translated Fiction in 2020 for *The Disaster Tourist*, while Hye-young Pyun's *The Hole* won the Shirley Jackson Prize in 2017.

I delighted too in discovering books by other male writers, including Un-su Kim's *The Plotters* (longlisted for the Dublin Prize in 2020), J.M. Lee's *The Investigation* and *Broken Summer*, and Bandi's *The Accusation*.

Today, the Korean books I have discovered and represented have been published in more than 40 countries, with many sold for film and TV adaptation.

Through Korean literature, I found a renewed motivation as a literary agent. I was deeply honoured to be given an award from the Korean Ministry of Culture for my work in 2016, followed by the London Book Fair's Literary Agent Award in 2017. Yet the greatest reward is every time a translated book of one of my authors arrives at my office. I love that feeling of excitement and discovery, opening a box posted from the other side of the world and finding the latest foreign edition to add to the shelves that line my office wall-to-wall. Korean literature is no longer unknown or strange. I have helped to give it the global recognition it deserves – one that is vibrant, diverse and profound. I am sure a Korean author will win the Nobel Prize for Literature one day soon.

After just a year of representing Korean books, I felt the country itself calling me. I set forth feeling like Indiana Jones – and I found the Lost Ark! The trip opened my eyes, heart and mind to the most fascinating, beautiful and inspiring people and landscapes I could ever imagine. Plus, there were no other Americans, no Brits, no Europeans, no tourists. I was the only blonde in a sea of dark-haired Koreans but I was made to feel completely at home.

I will never forget my first retreat in a Buddhist temple, high up in the mountains near Incheon. It sums up everything that made me fall in love with Korea. At the time, I was very anxious about my husband's recent health scare and his need for a life-saving transplant. While taking tea with a Buddhist monk, I found myself in tears. The monk looked directly at me and said, "We are happy now." He spoke firmly, so firmly, in fact, that I went from tears to laughter in a millisecond. "We are happy now" is what has motivated my own spiritual and mental transformation over the years. I have learned how to appreciate nature and simplicity, and how to be unconditionally supportive. I have learned that deep, forever pain is part of life but it can be subdued and transformed into motivation and contentment. Most importantly, I have found a renewed sense of happiness and energy.

"We are happy now" is a choice we can make, no matter the circumstances, and it has become my mantra.

·········

Korea is a miracle, and I don't use that word lightly. In fact, it is known as "the miracle on the Han River" for its incredible transformation from one of the poorest nations to one of the richest in the world.

Their history of the last century begins with so much conflict and pain: the occupation by Japan in 1910, the partition of 1945, the war in 1950 and finally the ongoing DMZ (Demilitarised Zone) marking the divide between North and South. By the mid-1950s, the country was one of the poorest on the planet, its economy predominantly based on agriculture. But in the last 70 years, Korea has rebuilt itself from the ground up through a combination of innovative government reforms, a high-quality education system and a dedicated, hardworking labour force. Its booming industries in cars, shipping, tech, electronics and yes, pop music, have transformed it into one of Asia's "tiger" economies and the tenth largest in the world.

Beyond being an economic powerhouse, Korea has what in Hollywood they call the "it" factor. Thanks to its prize-winning books, films, television and music, today Korean culture is on everyone's radar. Whether you are in London, New York, Stockholm or Tokyo and you have seen the K-pop bands BTS and Blackpink, or the dramas *Squid Game* and *Parasite*, you are experiencing *hallyu* – the "Korean wave".

The work ethic and fortitude of the Korean people are an inspiration. Yet I learned, as you will, that this progress and accomplishment is also due to something that goes beyond hard work and national pride, a secret that lies centuries deep.

The soul of Korea and the secret to its success and happiness is down to the people's devotion to the Confucian values of family, community, harmony and ritual, as well as the philosophies of *han, heung* and *jeong* – resilience, joy and the art of giving. These philosophies, born of the culture and often referenced in traditional Korean stories, poems, and music, make up the DNA of Korean life.

Han is difficult to define as it is a highly subjective term with many interpretations. It is both a celebration of grit, a reverence for effort and persistence, as well as a feeling of melancholy arising from a history of occupation, war and the separation of North and South. Koreans recognise that in life we can experience intense personal and national struggles, and that deep sorrow should be acknowledged.

A Korean friend summed it up this way: "*Han* is not just a feeling of pain and suffering; it is the energy that propelled Korea forward after the war, and in that sense it was a positive. It transformed us."

Heung is that incredible feeling of joy you experience at family gatherings, being out in nature, enjoying a cup of pine needle tea, or reading a great book.

And *jeong* is the art of giving without expecting anything in return, of prioritising the wellbeing of your family, friends, community and country, along with your own. It's loyalty and community. *Jeong* is the invisible thread that binds us all together.

·········

Korea has called me back many times, and each time I have explored and experienced new wonders, made new friends and deepened my relationship with the country and myself. I have been extraordinarily lucky to have my friend and author Kyung-sook Shin take me to places tourists rarely see, destinations I can now share with you. Each trip, each encounter, in Korea positively changed my life, and I hope reading about it might have a wonderful effect on you too.

Through these pages I invite you to take a trip with me to soak up the majesty and splendour of a country forged by grit, joy and a strong sense of community. We will travel from the vibrant capital Seoul, to meet with Buddhist nuns in the mountains; we will walk through the spy tunnels at the DMZ; explore the tropical island of Jeju, home to the inspirational octogenarian female divers, *haenyeo*; and share a big pot of delicious ginseng chicken soup sitting on straw mats on the floor of a restaurant surrounded by lotus flower fields.

After experiencing each new destination, you will learn the lessons that will make your life happier and more fulfilling, as they have mine. To finish off each chapter, I have included a mouth-watering traditional Korean recipe, kindly provided by some of my Korean friends for you to cook and enjoy.

I hope you will become enchanted by the beauty I have found in Korea and be inspired to visit too.

Enjoy the trip!

Destination:
Seoul

Greetings and Communication

인사말 그리고 소통

Insamal geurigo sotong

Welcome to Seoul, the hottest city in Asia

Seoul feels like a mash-up of New York, Hong Kong, Paris, London, Shanghai and Tokyo. It's a city of paradoxes: one of the most bustling, modern cities in the world while also ancient and full of green spaces of tranquillity. Futuristic skyscrapers sit beside age-old Buddhist temples, forests of neon signs, highways, underpasses and overpasses sprawl out among mountains and rivers. With over 10 million inhabitants, the traffic never stops, the energy never dwindles. Seoul is the pumping heart of Korea, the capital where everything is happening.

Here you can eat the best dumplings in the world, shop like you never have before and learn how a Korean massage and snail facial can change your life. You can visit nature in all its glory walking among the cherry blossoms along the Han River, without ever leaving the city.

On my first visit to Seoul, given I knew little about Korea other than its books, I decided to make the Westin Chosun Hotel my base of operations. Surrounded by embassies, royal palaces, Buddhist temples and majestic mountains, the Chosun is not just South Korea's most historic hotel but also its most iconic. Built in 1914, it was designed as a luxury European-style hotel, with a royal suite, a crystal chandelier from Tiffany's and Irish linen bedsheets. Presidents and dignitaries have stayed there; Marilyn Monroe visited. It was the height of sophistication, beauty and serenity then, and today it still is – although in a different guise, since most of the original four-storey building was demolished in the late 60s. The old-world glamour has been replaced by a modern, elegant five-star hotel: its marble-floored lobby bursting with floral arrangements, picture windows looking out from the bedrooms onto tranquil gardens and a Buddhist shrine, and – my favourite feature – a wonderful spa, where I experienced the most heavenly massage.

The minute I walked into the Chosun, my heartbeat slowed and I relaxed. Seoul is a bustling city, and the hotel provided me with instant respite, combining traditional Korean charm with modern luxury.

While I was there, I needed to entertain both the press and my authors, and there seemed no better place for this. The smart and incredibly accommodating staff helped me plan and arrange everything, from drinks with authors to an overnight stay at the oldest temple in the country and a trip to the demilitarised zone. Very quickly, the hotel had become my personal assistant, and then something deeper: it became my portal to Korea…

Within walking distance of the hotel sits Deoksugung Palace, one of five grand palaces built by the kings of Korea's Joseon dynasty, who ruled from 1392 to 1910. You can walk through the many buildings that make up the Deoksugung Palace: the banquet pavilion, the Jeukjodang Hall (rebuilt following a fire), where the kings were crowned, and then cross the famed

Geumcheongyo Bridge; built in 1411, it is the oldest surviving in Seoul. Three times a day in front of the Daehanmun Gate, there is a changing of the royal guard, which re-enacts the ceremony that took place during the early Joseon era (often compared to the changing of the guard at Buckingham Palace) – it is a must-see. Wearing traditional royal uniforms in bold blue, red and yellow and carrying flags, the guards march to the sound of rousing horns and drums. After some parading, the two shifts of guards exchange a password for verification before ending with some dramatic drumming and bellowing of orders as they swap positions. It is a great opportunity to experience a historical scene.

But the palace is not just for tourists; it's become a favourite destination for Korean women to connect with their heritage by dressing up in their traditional costume, *hanbok* – a short jacket tied with a ribbon and a colourful, long billowing skirt worn over five to seven layers of undergarments. For me, this reverence for the past through dress personifies the art of *heung* (joy) and *jeong* (community). (See Chapter 9 for how the *hanbok* is being incorporated into current fashion trends.)

Moments from Deoksugung Palace you can find its counterpoint: retailer Lotte's flagship store – think Harrods times a thousand! This was my introduction to Korean luxury shopping and opulent lifestyles, the perfect embodiment of the country's modern economic success.

On that first trip to Seoul, I was on a whirlwind of new sensations every hour of every day. All my senses were stimulated by the city: the smells wafting from kitchens, the aromas from the exotic teas, the sounds of Buddhist gongs reverberating amid the traffic and buzz of humanity. I found having a beautiful, serene home to return to every night gave me the energy and confidence to be adventurous in exploring the city.

The Westin Chosun Seoul
Address: 106, Sogong-ro, Jung-gu, Seoul
Website: www.echosunhotel.com

Deoksugung Palace
Address: Sejong-daero 99, Jung-gu, Seoul
Website: www.deoksugung.go.kr

Menage à trois

If, like me, you visit Korea without being able to speak Korean, you will experience a linguistic *menage à trois*. Since most Koreans do not speak English, or any other language for that matter. In this regard, Korea seems unusual; even its most famous writers, along with the majority of the publishing community, do not speak English.

When I travel with Kyung-sook Shin, she always invites a friend of hers along to interpret. It is the same with all my authors. An interpreter makes the conversation seamless, there are no misunderstandings and it also adds a fun factor. Three is a party!

When my novel *The J.M. Barrie Ladies' Swimming Society* was published in Korea, I was invited to speak at an event in Gunpo, a city that promotes book reading culture. Anton Hur, a young English-speaking interpreter was hired to accompany me. I was impressed by his ability to translate my speech since I am a fast talker – a New Yorker down to my bones!

On the drive back to Seoul, I learned that Anton was also a literary translator and asked if he was interested in translating Kyung-sook's book *The Court Dancer*. Anton confessed Kyung-sook was his idol and jumped at the chance. It turned out to be the beginning of a beautiful relationship and since then he has translated all her books. Today, he is probably the most famous translator of Korean literature, shortlisted for the International Booker Prize, as well as a novelist in his own right.

While I think it's a good idea if you are going to Korea to have a translator by your side, these days, communication has been made much easier thanks to Google Translate. I often find shopkeepers take out their phones and ask me to speak into them – seconds later my questions are translated into Korean.

Google Translate has become an incredible tool when travelling in Korea, or anywhere really, but I still prefer a human being!

Etiquette lessons

Before you can really experience Seoul and Korea, it's important to understand its customs and etiquette, some of which date back 5000 years and are steeped in the Confucian principles of respect for elders and community harmony. Although Koreans will generally accept any cultural faux pas made by visitors, it is much better to be informed so you can make a good impression. Trust me on this – I learned the hard way!

I once arranged an early-morning Zoom meeting with a very important Korean publisher. I was in New York and had to wake up at 5am for the call. After drinking lots of coffee and putting on a business suit and make-up, I was ready. My Korean associate, Sue, acted as the interpreter. The meeting lasted almost an hour. I thought it went well, that I had established a good rapport for future business. Later, to my horror, Sue received a letter from the publisher suggesting I had been rude and that she would never do business with me. I was flabbergasted. I thought it had gone brilliantly!

Sue understood what had happened. She explained that in conversation, I am animated and gesticulate with my hands a lot. (I am not Italian, but I could be!) She told me that waving hands when talking is insulting in Korean culture, and by doing so, I had inadvertently disrespected the publisher. Apologies were offered and everything was smoothed over, but I learned a lesson I won't forget.

Sometimes, miscommunication in Korea can lead to major consequences. Several years ago, I agreed to represent a harrowing and poetic book, *The*

Accusation, by a North Korean using the pseudonym Bandi. It was a collection of short stories about the lives of ordinary people under the dictatorship. Written in secret between 1989 and 1995, the book was smuggled out of the country in 2013. The people who facilitated this cannot be identified for security reasons. But I did have the honour of meeting the North Korean woman (who had escaped to the South) and was now translating the book from North Korean dialect. (She divulged how North Korean culture has been frozen in time since the war.)

We enjoyed a wonderful meal along with my Korean agent and publishers. I elected myself as party photographer. I was so overcome with excitement that before going to bed, I sent a photo to my husband and sister. The next morning, my husband called from New York. He told me that my sister had woken him in the middle of the night in a panic, worried that I might post the pictures on social media. (I had not.)

"Barbara will get herself killed! The North Koreans will be after her. Tell her not to post any pictures on Facebook or any social media."

I laughed at her typical over-reaction and texted that I hadn't posted anywhere. She was already upset that I was handling the book, nervous that my life could be in peril.

Later I told my Korean agent what had happened, and he agreed it would have been dangerous to post the images, as the translator's family was in North Korea and could become a target. Sometimes posting on social media can have real-life costs. Given we all live our lives online, it's only natural to want to share and post in the moment. But it's still important to check first.

Koreans are very willing to meet you more than halfway if you don't speak the language. When my friend Gabriella and I made a trip to attend the Seoul Book Fair, we decided to explore an area of the city unknown to us. For lunch, we found a tiny, modest café run by three generations of Korean women, with the grandmother standing over a huge pot and continuously stirring. It felt perfectly authentic. There was one problem: we do not speak

Korean and the menu had no English translation. This was before Google translate was up and running. It was only as we were being handed the menu that Gabriella reminded me that she was deathly allergic to fish. Many Korean dishes are made with a fish sauce, so this was serious. How were we going to explain it to our hosts? It was time to summon all my communication skills.

Picture this: I am pretending to be a fish, my arms extended as if I am swimming, my eyes and mouth opened wide. I move my hand in a line over my neck as if I am cutting my throat and then I collapse dramatically onto the floor. "No fish." I say, "Fish kills."

Gabriella is in hysterics, the waitress is laughing, and now Grandma chef has come to watch.

It wasn't an Oscar-winning performance, but after everyone had stopped laughing, the women nodded; they understood perfectly. They appreciated my effort and weren't insulted that I didn't speak Korean. Shortly after, they served us a delicious bowl of noodles filled with lots of green vegetables. We not only made some wonderful friends there that day, but Gabriella ate healthfully and didn't end up in hospital!

Learning to communicate (or improvise) is as critical as your passport in any country you visit. But the stakes can be higher in Korea because the customs and etiquette woven into daily life there are more elaborate than what you may be familiar with.

So whether you are going to Korea as a tourist or for business, mastering the customs is not just a sign of respect; it's your first key to the country.

And it all starts with the bow.

Learn to bow the Korean way

I learned how to bow by knocking my head and nearly getting a concussion.

Behind a stone gate in the grounds of the Chosun Hotel lies a beautiful garden containing the octagonal Hwangudan Altar complex, a designated historic site. A three-storey shrine sits atop a granite base guarded by over a dozen stone fire-eating creatures known as *haetae*. It was constructed in 1897 by the newly self-proclaimed Emperor Gojong, of the short-lived Daehan Empire, to perform the "rites of heaven" to ensure a bountiful harvest. Next to the shrine are three enormous stone drums, intricately carved with dragons (a reference to the drums used in the ceremonial rites).

I walked over to the garden and, probably due to jet lag, hit my head on the stone arch of the entrance gate. I had to stand for a moment and catch my breath as an elderly man was trying to exit. He saw what had happened and, after waiting patiently, introduced himself, offering to show me how to approach and enter the altar complex, a sacred place.

He explained that to show respect I must perform a small bow before entering. He demonstrated how: placing his arms alongside his body and bending his torso horizontally. "Your head should never be higher than the heavens," he added.

That was the beginning of my education about Korean customs and etiquette. The tradition of bowing, *jeol*, is centuries old and very important. It is incorporated into all aspects of life as a sign of respect and as a greeting; it is the way to enter a room, say hello, goodbye and see you later, and when someone bows to you, you always bow in return.

The different levels of bowing

If you are meeting a friend, tilt your head down slightly.

For business colleagues or your superiors, bow your head lower, to show greater respect.

The *keunjeol* (big bow) is the most formal and deepest bow, given typically to older family members at ceremonies and on festival days. When meeting a religious figure like a monk, put your hands together in prayer as you bow.

After the bow, comes the greeting!

The greeting

In Korea, social etiquette is more formal than in most Western countries. Address people by their professional titles unless they ask you to use their names. (Korean names are the reverse of Western names, with the surname coming first.)

Be careful with physical greetings. It is not done to give a single or double kiss on the cheek when meeting a friend or colleague; nor should you hug or pat someone on the back. Instead, you can shake hands, but how you shake depends on the age or status of the person you are meeting. (Please note, Korean women do not shake hands, but nod lightly.) A person will shake with one hand when greeting someone of lower status than themself. To show respect to someone of higher status than yourself, use your left hand to support your right arm as you shake. One tip is to use both hands when first meeting someone.

If you are meeting Koreans in a work setting, after the bow and greeting comes the exchange of business cards. This is significant in setting up the relationship with your new colleague, as it gives them information about your title and position in a company.

Always accept the card with two hands and read it for a few seconds before putting it down in front of you at a table. (Don't put it away.)

How old are you?

Pretty soon after you arrive in Korea you will be asked a question that you are neither expecting nor keen to answer.

On my first trip to Korea, I flew fourteen and a half hours from New York City to Seoul – and that's not counting the hours spent going through security, customs and waiting for my luggage. By the time I arrived at my hotel, I felt like I hadn't slept for three days. To this day, I can't believe I made it out of the taxi and into the hotel lobby.

Waiting for me with flowers were two young associates from a literary organisation. They had come to personally welcome me to Seoul. It was a beautiful gesture that I would have appreciated more if I hadn't wanted to lie down on the marble floor and fall asleep on the spot. I could barely talk.

I thanked them for the flowers and said goodbye, but they insisted on helping me up to my room, carrying my bags, even my handbag. What could I do?

En route to my room, they asked me this question.

"How old are you?"

"Excuse me?" I answered. "What??? Am I hearing correctly? Did you just ask me my age??!"

I could feel adrenaline pulsing through my veins. Were they kidding me? I had woken up completely. My voice rose a few decibels. "Are you absolutely out of your minds? There are two questions you NEVER ask a woman," I told them. "'How old are you?' and 'How much do you weigh?'"

Fear shooting out of their eyeballs, they looked like they were going to cry. I realised that my New York attitude might be too much for them.

"I am so sorry I yelled but I'm exhausted…" I offered.

They explained in a very serious tone that it is customary to ask someone's age so they can show respect and address you properly. Korean etiquette dictates different rules for those older and younger than oneself.

I listened politely and then burst out laughing. "Forget all that. Just call me Barbara!"

They were so relieved I wasn't angry, but I think they found it difficult to call me by my first name as I was much older than they were. However, I insisted that from then on, everyone I met should call me Barbara and that was it.

I always respect Korean traditions, but I have also taught my Korean friends about my casual New York style and they have accepted my way too. Once they knew it was really okay.

"Very difficult, very difficult"

Koreans don't like saying no; they consider it rude. They wouldn't want to disappoint anyone. They also go to great pains to avoid giving the wrong answer and possibly lose face. I learned this when the writer Han Kang (my client at the time) invited me to a very special art exhibition to celebrate the publication of her novel, *The White Book*.

The show was being held in a tiny gallery down a brick alley in the old quarter of Seoul. This alley was so narrow, two people could not walk side by side. Being the voluptuous, New York woman I am, I worried about getting stuck between the alley walls. The entrance was behind carved wooden doors, and I felt I was being led towards a secret hideaway. The exhibition itself was very emotional, about life, death, war and loss. Naturally, I encouraged some of Han Kang's European publishers, also in Seoul, to visit the show. I asked my Korean agent for the address and he promised to get it.

After not hearing from him, I called to follow up.

"The publishers are leaving tomorrow and they want to go to the show today," I explained.

His reply?

"Very difficult, very difficult."

"I don't understand. What does that mean?" I asked.

"Very difficult, very difficult," came a second reply.

I simply couldn't understand what was so complicated about getting the gallery's address. He promised to contact Kang and find out.

Finally, late that night he called to say Kang also said, "very difficult".

I thought this was complete madness. What could be so difficult? Had I imagined the whole thing? Did the art gallery really exist?

"What is the problem? Is it a magic place like in a Harry Potter movie?" I kidded.

The response?

"Very difficult, very difficult."

I had come across this mysterious address amnesia every time I was invited anywhere in Seoul; I'd be given multiple addresses to give the cab driver. I found all this baffling but I was so busy that I just thought, this is Seoul – go with it.

A few days after the exhibition, J.M. Lee, one of the most famous authors in the country and a client of mine, invited me and my Korean agent to a beautiful dinner. Once again, we drove around for what seemed like hours until we reached the restaurant. Going home, J.M. asked if there was anything he could do for me while I was visiting. I told him about the art gallery drama and needing two addresses to get anywhere. Was I crazy or was something going on? *The Matrix* made more sense to me than Seoul! I cried.

He started laughing deeply. "Oh, the addresses! Yes. It's crazy. I'll tell you everything." He then explained that ten years prior, the government had changed all the street numbers, names and addresses in the entire city of Seoul. The idea was to modernise the capital, but the result was a kind of chaos that nobody wanted to talk about.

Many streets had never previously had numbers or addresses; they were just known by surrounding landmarks. Streets with existing names were given new ones. It would be like changing Park Avenue in New York to Barbara Street. No wonder no one knew where they were going.

Aside from how crazy this seemed to me, it was also unbelievable that no one had told me before. Very often you won't find answers to your questions in Korea. It can feel like a tangled web of confusion. But that's part of the fun of it, if you understand this from the start. I love a good mystery, so Seoul is the city for me.

Every day is Christmas in Korea

Giving gifts is one of the key elements of a greeting in Korea. It's a way to convey respect, keep good *kibun* (a good state of mind) and show modest graciousness. It is as essential as bowing or saying hello.

In Korea, gift giving is not just for holidays; it is an everyday ritual – and the presentation is as important as the gift itself. Whether you are seeing a long-time client, friend or meeting someone for the first time, bringing a gift is vital. It is a lovely way to break the ice and make the other person feel respected and appreciated. Similarly, always bring a gift when invited into someone's home. To come empty-handed is considered rude and thoughtless.

The cost of the gift doesn't matter; it is the thought and care that goes into it that counts. It's a good idea to wrap gifts in either the royal colours of red and yellow, blue for luck, or pink and yellow for happiness. (Don't sign a card or letter in red ink – it means you are ending a relationship.)

For major life events, Koreans will go all out. A baby's "first" birthday, *dol* or *doljanchi*, is a big celebration. In Korea, your age is not what it is any-where else in the world. Korean babies turn one the day they are born (their first year starts at conception) and they turn two the year that we would traditionally think of as the first birthday. Which is when they celebrate the *doljanchi*. A party is held in the child's honour with rice cakes (signifying good luck), seaweed soup (to honour mothers who traditionally eat the soup post-partum) and fruits. The highlight of the *doljanchi* is the *doljabi*, a game to reveal the baby's future. Parents lay out six to eight items, including coins (wealth), books (intelligence) and yarn (longevity) on a table or tray. The baby picks two items, and these choices are said to map out their life path.

While gifts of gold rings were once given, today, money is the conventional gift. Money is also given at wedding celebrations and other birthdays. For a 60th, 70th or 80th birthday, alcohol or gift baskets are also appropriate. And if you are invited to a housewarming, forget the candle or coffee maker. In Korea, typical gifts for those moving into a new home are cleaning products and toilet paper!

Reciprocity is also a crucial part of the culture in Korea. It's best not to give expensive gifts, as the recipient will feel obligated to reciprocate with a gift of equal value.

Gifts are given and received with two hands, just like business cards. Also, never immediately open a present when given it – unwrap it later.

Barbara's Korean candy store

The first time I went to Seoul, I knew that I should bring gifts for everyone, but I wasn't sure exactly what to buy. In the airport duty-free shop, I found what I was looking for: boxes of See's Candies, a very American brand that was popular when I was a child. My mother and grandmother used to gift See's Candies when they were invited for dinner, so the candy had a sentimental and special meaning to me.

Since I wanted to give a gift to everyone I was meeting for business, I bought 60 boxes! I stacked them into a tower in my hotel room and every time I was due to meet someone, I would take a box. Yet one evening, when meeting an associate at my hotel bar, I had forgotten to bring their gift. I ran upstairs to my room, grabbed two boxes and returned.

"Do you have a candy store in your room?" my associate asked, amazed and delighted.

"Yes!" I confessed.

Everyone loved the candy, particularly as it had a story attached to it that had a connection to me. This in turn made it meaningful for them.

When you visit Korea, bring gifts that are truly personal if you can. Another time, I brought two of my clients horseshoes from a cowboy store in Kansas City – they were so authentic, I think they still had dirt on them. My clients had both moved to new homes, and I wanted to give them horseshoes to hang over their doorways for good luck. When I explained the meaning to them, they were so grateful.

Love is always in the air

South Koreans celebrate Valentine's Day on 14 February, yet there is a twist: only women give a gift – usually chocolate – to their significant other. But don't worry, there are plenty of other opportunities to lavish gifts on loved ones and spend time with them. In fact, there are twelve holidays every year when Koreans celebrate romance, always on the fourteenth of the month. My favourites are:

14 March is White Day, when men give gifts to their girlfriends, most often white chocolates or white flowers.

14 April is Black Day, when singles who did not receive gifts in February or March meet up and celebrate singledom by proudly wearing black and

eating noodles with a black bean sauce – *jjajangmyeon*. In Korea, life is completely marriage and family centric so to have a day that recognises single people is wonderful.

14 May is Rose Day, which sees lovers giving each other yellow roses, while singles wear yellow, eat yellow curry and resolve to find a lover!

Korea's Thanksgiving

The two biggest holidays in Korea are: Seollal or Lunar New Year, celebrating the first day of the Korean lunar calendar, and Chuseok, which can be thought of as Korea's Thanksgiving. Chuseok is a three-day holiday when people return to their hometowns to celebrate the harvest with their families and honour ancestors with memorial ceremonies.

Gifts are an important part of the celebration and typically they are ones that families can share: fruit baskets, gift sets of special teas or Korean candies, wellness gifts for senior family members or traditional sweet treats such as *songpyeon* – rice cakes stuffed with sweetened sesame seed fillings – and *gwapyeon*, a fruit jelly prepared from an assortment of Korean cherries, quinces, apricot and hawthorn boiled with starch and honey. It's believed to have been first served in the royal courts of the Joseon dynasty.

The most unusual gift I ever received while visiting Korea was from an author I represent. It was an embroidered buckwheat-hull pillow. Once I learned that it is meant to improve your sleep and digestion – a gift of good health – I was really touched by the thoughtfulness.

Lessons from Korean greetings and communication

- Communication is key to our lives. Be respectful of every-one you meet – this will lead to your success in every social encounter.
- Reciprocity is a cornerstone of Korean culture. Make sure the value of the gift you give can be afforded in return without causing financial stress.
- The true value of gift giving is the thought behind it. Bring a unique gift from your country that has meaning and a story attached.
- Always practise the local etiquette – this shows respect and esteem for your hosts.
- Being honest with others, even if it may be uncomfortable, builds trust and enables you to sustain authentic relationships.

Beef Dumplings

고기만두

(Gogimandu)

My friend Kyung-sook Shin, author of *Please Look After Mom*, gave me this recipe, which I have eaten at her home on many visits.

"Koreans make steamed dumplings or dumpling soup from scratch on big holidays such as Chuseok or Seol. Dumplings are tricky to make, so we tend to make an ample amount in one sitting to fill the freezer, and make use of its precious stock in the coming weeks or months.

"Every family has a different recipe, but each dumpling is usually named after its key ingredient. Ones with an overwhelming presence of kimchi will be called kimchi dumplings, those with tofu, tofu dumplings, and those filled with meat, meat dumplings, and so forth.

"It's safe to say that, in all my life, I have never met

anyone who dislikes dumplings, Korean or not.

"Barbara can vouch for this. On one of her visits, I served her dumpling soup using dumplings prepared by my sister-in-law. Barbara wolfed it all down.

"Dumplings are one of those dishes that bring smiles to people's eyes. I think it is because they look somewhat endearing to begin with. And even better, most dumplings are small enough for anyone to try one or two without feeling too intimidated.

"Dumplings happen to be one of my favorite foods. Whenever I have moved house in the past, I have always quickly sought out and became a regular at the neighborhood's best dumpling place.

"Really, I recommend any traveller who ends up in Korea to try any dumpling place in any neighborhood, because, I promise, you'll be surprised how good it is – no matter which restaurant you walk into. My mouth waters just thinking about the delicious smell of dumplings when I open the steamer."

Ingredients
(Serves 5)

Broth
Handful of sea tangle (seaweed)
Handful of dried prawns
Handful of dried anchovies

Dough
250g flour
115g rice flour
3 tbsp sticky rice flour
½ tsp salt
1 egg white
200ml warm water

Stuffing
75g bean sprouts
75g glass noodles
225g minced beef
100g tofu, chopped
1 tbsp garlic paste
1 tsp sesame oil
Pinch of black pepper
½ tsp salt
1 tbsp rice flour
1 egg yolk
Korean-style soy sauce

1. The night before, prepare the broth. Fill a large pot with cold water and throw in a handful of sea tangle, dried prawns and dried anchovies (for vegans, you can omit this). Leave it to infuse overnight. (Or for ease, you can use chicken stock.)

2. To make the dumplings, mix all the flours and salt together in a bowl, then add the egg white and combine to form a dough.

3. Knead the dough while adding the water little by little, until it feels elastic and smooth.

4. Once the dough's ready, wrap it in clingfilm and let it sit for 5–6 hours in the fridge.

5. To prepare the stuffing, briefly steam the bean sprouts for 1 minute and then the glass noodles for 3 minutes (or follow the packet instructions). Pat them dry and chop them into little pieces.

6. In a bowl, mix the sprouts and noodles with the minced beef and tofu. Add the garlic paste, sesame oil, pepper, salt, rice flour and egg yolk and combine thoroughly.

7. Now put the stuffing aside, while you prepare the dumpling wrappers. Remove the dough from the fridge. You might need to let it

stand for 5 minutes to allow it to soften up and become more malleable.

8. Break off a palm-sized amount of dough and, using a rolling pin, roll it out on a clean, floured surface to make a thin circle of about 12cm in diameter. Repeat until there is no dough left, sprinkling a bit of flour on both sides of each dumpling wrapper to prevent them sticking to the work surface.

9. To make spherical dumplings, place a small ball of stuffing in the middle of a circle of dough, then pull the sides around it, pressing the edges together at the centre like a stem; or for empanada-shaped dumplings, place the stuffing on one half of the dough circle, fold the other half over and press the edges together to form a seal.

10. Bring your broth to a rolling boil, stir in some garlic paste. Next add the dumplings, along with some soy sauce.

11. When the dumplings start to rise to the top of the pot and look translucent (5–10 minutes depending on the size) they should be done. To check, pierce them with a chopstick. If it goes through cleanly, they are ready.

12. Spoon the soup into bowls and sprinkle over some garnishes: either an omelette cut into strips or some diced raw or dried mushrooms.

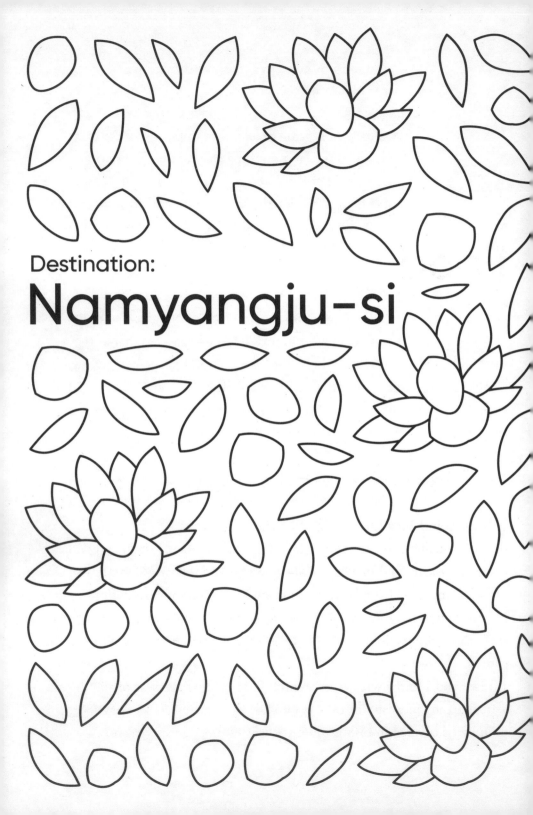

Destination:
Namyangju-si

Food

음식

Eumsik

The soup and the lotus

When I'm in Korea I have so many authors, publishers and editors to meet that it's usually impossible to take a day off. So when Joseph, my Korean co-agent, asked if I'd like to get out of Seoul and go for a drive to the city of Namyangju-si, I jumped at the chance. A 25-minute trip from Seoul, Namyangju-si is home to a movie studio complex (with a replica DMZ set for filming), walking trails, royal Joseon tombs and an ecological water garden.

Little did I know what was in store. I sat in the back seat of the car and watched the landscape change from city to countryside, as we drove into mountains covered in lush greenery. It was summer and it was hot.

After an hour or so, we arrived at the outskirts of Namyangju-si, where Joseph turned off the main road and parked the car. We walked along a dirt track to a little restaurant, outside of which people were gathered around a picnic table underneath a clump of huge trees. We stepped through an entrance into an old stone courtyard where a squawking chicken ran around in circles while a sunbathing little dog barely gave us a glance. We came to the doorway of a small dining room, where we removed our shoes before going inside and sitting, in the traditional Korean style, on straw mats on the floor, around a low table. The waiter brought out little dishes of kimchi, lotus roots, radishes and pickles, then lit the stove in the centre of the table. On this, he placed a large stone pot containing chicken stuffed with rice, ginseng, garlic and jujube, cooked in broth.

This was Korea's famous *samgyetang* – ginseng chicken soup. The dish is believed to strengthen your immune system and stimulate your mind. It is eaten all year round, but particularly in summer, when it is said to boost your body weakened from sweating all season.

I think chicken soup is the ultimate comfort food, and every culture has its own version – from the Greek *avgolemono* with lemon, to the Jewish "penicillin" with matzo balls.

In Korea, ginseng chicken soup is not just about the soup – it's a bowl of friendship, love, comfort, joy and gratitude. And so it was with my first bowl. Sharing a big pot with my friends made for an unforgettable experience. Although I was thousands of miles from home, the soup was familiar and instantly comforting. It reminded me of my grandma's chicken soup but with a special twist from the ginseng and Korean vegetables that made it very much its own.

After lunch, we took a long stroll to a lotus field, a heart-stopping sight; a sea of pink flowers swaying in the summer breeze.

The lotus is one of the most important symbols in Korean culture. It grows in muddy water and sends up shoots to bloom above the surface with extraordinary beauty. A flower that blossoms unscathed despite its surroundings is something we can all learn from; it's a metaphor that has inspired people for centuries. In both Confucianism and Buddhism, the lotus symbolises virtue, purity of heart and spiritual awakening.

I remember that, at the time, I could not believe that here I was in Namyangju-si, experiencing two of the great wonders of Korea – mother nature in all her beauty, and the best ginseng chicken soup in the world!

Bap Meogeosseoyo?

The first thing any person will ask you whether in the office, on a date or at home is "*Bap meogeosseoyo?*" It literally means "Have you eaten"? But it also doubles up as "How are you?" After centuries of starvation and poverty, wars and famine, in Korea, every meal is considered precious. Over my extended visits, I learned that feeding a friend, guest, family member or a stranger is fundamental to being Korean.

But I also learned this: in Korea a meal is never just about the food. It's about the people and their culture, their relationship to nature and history. My understanding of Korean people began through the meals I enjoyed with them. In Korea, every breakfast, lunch and dinner is an occasion: to be grateful, to share and to enjoy delicious, healthy food. This makes dining etiquette an important practice of daily life. It's all about creating harmony and respect around the table, a beautiful custom, and it is essential for a guest to master.

Whether you were a member of the royal family who ruled Korea for centuries, or a village farmer, historically, eating was a communal experience. This custom persists today: an illustration of *jeong*, the invisible thread binding Koreans together.

Korean culture also places the elderly at the top of the social hierarchy, so everyone must wait for the oldest person at the table to sit first and start eating first. (This is another reason why Koreans ask your age.)

Shoes are removed when entering restaurants and private homes (so make sure you have clean feet or socks). In many traditional restaurants, you will dine sitting on the floor. And it is also good to know that there is no tipping.

The preparation of food is a long process and the presentation is always a delicate art. The staples of any Korean meal include rice, noodles, kimchi, tofu, garlic, ginger, chilli paste, pickled vegetables and roots, along with fish, pork, beef or chicken. Protein is used sparingly – no one in Korea eats an entire rib-eye steak. Instead, that steak would be sliced thinly and served in moderate portions along with other fresh ingredients. Not a whiff of French fries or processed foods! And you won't find salt and pepper on any table, nor bread and butter. Salads, fruits, vegetables and roots are all arranged on platters and plates as if they were flowers.

Unlike the Chinese or Japanese, Koreans have used spoons since the fifth century, as well as metal (not wooden) chopsticks. It is a faux pas to stand your chopsticks upright in your bowl of rice – this gesture is reserved for ceremonies honouring ancestors when rice bowls are given up as offerings. Instead, you should rest them on the edge of your plate.

Koreans feed their guests very well. I have been privileged to be hosted warmly by clients for lunches and dinners. If invited into someone's home for a meal, Koreans will say "*Jal meokkesseumnida*", which translates as "I will eat well", before starting. "Thank you for the meal" is "*Jal meogeosseumnida*" and is how you show appreciation to your host.

Meals are never rushed, allowing everyone to savour their food and the company. I learned that traditionally there is no main course; instead, there are *banchan* – many little dishes of steamed, pickled, boiled or fried vegetables that are replenished throughout the lunch or dinner. Everyone partakes of everything and shares. And no one overfills their plate – in fact, it is considered rude to leave food on it. They take small amounts of food repeatedly until they are full. A delicious soup ends the meal.

Food is never wasted or thrown out. An important lesson I have learned from many Korean meals is to eat slowly and in small portions for better digestion. I believe this way of eating is the path to maintaining a healthy weight.

Korean food A–Z

The Korean language is not easy to learn for most visitors. It has a different alphabet – *hangul* – and the syntax is unique. But after my first Korean meal, I quickly learned what to ask for. When I am hungry for glass noodles, I say *japchae*. When I'm desperate for some dumplings, I can say *mandu*. So here is my list of food to eat when visiting Korea – learn these words and you'll never go hungry.

Bibimbap – leftover love

Bibimbap, which translates as "rice mish-mash", is a popular meal in Korean homes. First eaten centuries ago by farmers, *bibimbap* is a bowl of rice topped with some meat, an egg and vegetables. A practical use for surplus food in your fridge, it is easy to make at home – take some rice, add in leftover *bulgogi*, seafood or chicken, soft-boil an egg, toss in some sliced spring onions and bean sprouts and voilà! – you have a balanced meal in a bowl.

Bulgogi – fire meat

Like most Americans, my introduction to Korean food was through Korean barbecue – *bulgogi*. Literally, the word means "fire meat". *Bulgogi* is thinly sliced beef marinated in a mix of soy sauce, ginger, garlic, sesame seeds, black pepper and onions. You can throw in some pineapple juice or other fruit or sugar to add a bit of sweetness.

Bulgogi is cooked over an open fire, usually on a grill set inside a table. Though usually made with beef, it can be done with chicken or seafood. (In Seoul, the best place to find a seafood barbecue restaurant is on Grilled Fish Street in Dongdaemun.)

The fun of eating Korean barbecue is that you cook it yourself. Platters of thinly sliced meat and dishes of kimchi, pickles and white rice are brought to the table, the meat is placed on the grill, and then they leave you to it. Once it has cooked, place a slice in your bowl of rice or wrap it in a lettuce leaf, spread some dipping sauce on it, and enjoy one of the best morsels of your life.

Cheers!

You will find many meals and celebrations in Korea are accompanied by a glass of *soju*, a spirit distilled from rice, barley, wheat and more recently, sweet potatoes. Often compared to vodka, *soju* is considered the national drink, and has a long history. Records date it to the thirteenth century, when Mongol invaders brought the distillation methods of arak, an alcoholic drink made of grapes and aniseed, to Korea.

Served in shot glasses, the rule of drinking *soju* is that you never pour for yourself and always use two hands when pouring for others. They will fill up your glass in return. The toast in Korea is "*geonbae!*" which means "cheers!" or "drain the glass!"

Chimaek

It was during the Korean War (1950–1953) that Koreans first tasted American-style fried chicken. The story goes that American troops stationed in South Korea were not able to have turkey on Thanksgiving and had fried chicken instead, sharing it with their South Korean allies. The Korean soldiers took a liking to this variation – previously chicken had always been steamed or boiled in Korea.

Fast-forward, and today, Korean fried chicken is one of the most popular foods in the country, either as a meal or a snack. In fact, a recent survey found Korean fried chicken also ranked number one among non-Koreans when asked their favourite Korean food. (Kimchi came second, and *bibimbap* came third.)

There is one big difference between Korean fried chicken and the Western recipe. In Korea, the chicken is fried twice to make the skin extra thin and crispy. You can buy your chicken pieces plain, or basted with spicy sauces containing chilli or garlic. No matter your preference, Korean fried chicken is always washed down with beer. So, the dish is known locally as *chimaek* ("*chi*" for chicken and "*maek*" for *maekju*, which is beer).

If you are hungry for fried chicken in Korea, you are spoiled for choice. There are an estimated 80,000 fried chicken restaurants in the country, many of them chains. And if you are outside Korea, also no problem! Many of the major Korean chains have now opened stores overseas.

Japchae – Korean pasta

Japchae is one of my favourite dishes. It consists of glass noodles made from either mung beans, sweet potatoes or other beans or vegetables, stir-fried with spring onions, carrots and other greens. The consistency is much lighter than pasta, but the noodles expertly soak up the sauce they are cooked in.

Kimchi – the national dish

If every country has a scent, then kimchi, a dish of salted and fermented vegetables, long considered the national food, must be it in Korea! When Queen Elizabeth II visited Korea in 1999 on a royal tour, a kimchi-making demonstration at the ancient village of Hahoe was part of her itinerary.

The history of kimchi can be traced back thousands of years to when Koreans used to preserve their vegetables for winter by fermenting them in earthenware jars buried in the earth. Crunchy and spicy, kimchi is a fantastic health food too, rich in fibre, vitamin C, probiotics and carotene (which is converted by the body into vitamin A).

Used as a flavouring, spice, appetizer, side dish or eaten alone, kimchi can be made in hundreds of different ways but the most popular is from cabbage, white radishes and cucumbers. The vegetables are soaked in a brine containing ginger, garlic, green onion and chilli pepper, and bottled to last for an entire season.

Making kimchi is like making jams or preserves – no one makes just one jar, it is a day-long process and should be done in large quantities. (Make your own kimchi following the recipe in Chapter 7.)

And in case you were wondering how important kimchi is to Korean culture, just know that in Seoul there is a kimchi museum.

Mandu – dumpling heaven

Korean dumplings are small bundles of scrumptious flavour eaten as appetisers, or in soups. Squares of dough are filled with vegetables, meat, seafood, onions, kimchi, spinach and just about anything else. I've provided a simple recipe for making dumplings from scratch with just rice flour on page 34 but you can also add mashed yams or spinach to the dough. *Mandu* can be either boiled in a broth to make a hearty soup, or fried or baked and served with soy sauce and a hint of vinegar, garlic, ginger or chilli.

Rice makes the world go round

Rice is a staple of every Korean table, but for Koreans it's much more than just a food. At one time, your wealth was determined by how much rice you had in storage. Rice is *ssal* in Korean. But once cooked, it's called *bap*.

On Korean New Year's Day, the first day of the Lunar calendar, families will eat *tteokguk*, a broth containing thin rice cakes, symbolising health and good luck.

Many people will buy rice cakes, but those who want a specific texture or mix of different grains will make their own, soaking the rice overnight in their homes, then taking it to a gristmill to be ground. The gristmill, usually located at a traditional marketplace, will also grind people's seeds into cooking oil. This is popular because it produces a much fresher oil and ensures that no artificial additives are added.

The real squid game

How adventurous are you when it comes to food? If you think you will try anything, a good test awaits you in Korea with *sannakji*. Also known as "wriggling octopus", it's a dish of raw, chopped baby octopus – and yes, it does actually wriggle. (The truth is this isn't because it is actually alive by the time it is served, but because the octopus' complicated nervous system causes the reflex action in the tentacles to persist even when they have no input from the brain.) It can be prepared with sesame oil or chilli paste and is eaten with chopsticks.

Lessons from a Korean table

- Chicken soup is the elixir of life.
- Drink lots of herbal teas, incorporate more vegetables into your meals and eat protein sparingly. You'll feel the health and wellness benefits immediately.
- Be adventurous, try something new like kimchi or ginseng-infused foods – or even wriggling octopus!

- Slow down and savour your meals. If you eat in a hurry, you can't taste your food. Take smaller portions and go back for seconds if you're still hungry. This way you can teach yourself to eat enough to be satisfied but not too much so you feel full.
- Eating with family and friends, even with your dog or cat by your side, will make you happier. Social bonding and communication are what keep us sane!
- Think of every day as a Thanksgiving day. Koreans are grateful for how far they have come as a country, and it's evident every time a traditional meal is prepared and served. So do make sure to give thanks and feel a sense of pride in yourself and your family, friends, country and the world – and make sure you enjoy your food too.

Korean Ginseng Chicken Soup

삼계탕

(Samgyetang)

This recipe is from Dongkyung Lee, the mother of my associate Sue Park, and an excellent cook. Unlike most soups, which are considered winter fare, this one is popular during the hazy days of the Korean summer.

"Ginseng chicken soup has multiple different names in Korea, such as *samgyetang* or *baeksook*. Unlike American chicken soup, Korean ginseng chicken soup is considered a summertime food, eaten particularly around the time of *sambok* – the season of the peninsula's heatwaves. Because of its simple yet strong and nutritious ingredients, this soup is believed to improve your health and prepare you for the brutal summer ahead. So it's become a summertime ritual for Koreans to have a bowl of this ginseng chicken soup.

"While it's now a common dish, and even a bit of a comfort food for most chicken-loving Koreans, when I was a little kid, we couldn't afford to eat this soup every summer. Back then, meat was still a rare commodity, and chickens were valuable assets that laid sellable eggs, so it was unthinkable to eat them.

"So it was only when I was in my twenties that I first ate chicken soup, around the time my mom started raising a whole horde of chickens and we could afford to eat it. In part because of my experience with this dish, and in part because of the elegant simplicity of it, I've always thought the heart of this soup is just a good, well-raised chicken boiled down to its hearty, meaty essence. So I revere this classic recipe above all others, where ginseng and garlic are the only other key ingredients enhancing the chicken's flavours. It truly needs nothing else."

Ingredients

(Serves 4-6)

250ml cup of sticky rice
2 ginseng roots
1 whole garlic bulb
1 whole chicken (1.5kg)
Black pepper
Salt

Garnishes

Korean seaweed sheet
Spring onions, finely sliced

Pine nuts, toasted

1. First, leave a 250ml cup of sticky rice in a pot full of lukewarm water for about 20 minutes in advance. This will allow the rice to soften and cook better within the chicken later.

2. While the rice is soaking, peel the ginseng and garlic – there's no need to chop them.

3. Stuff the chicken with the sticky rice, ginseng and garlic.

4. Put the chicken in a large stock pot, breast side up, and cover it with water.

5. Put the lid on and place the pot over a high heat to bring it to the boil. Then turn down the heat and allow it to simmer for 45–50 minutes.

6. Turn off the stove, but don't open the pot yet. Leave it sitting for ten minutes – this process will make the chicken more tender and bring the flavours to their full potential.

7. Carefully remove the chicken from the pot and place on a carving board with ridges to collect the juices. Using a knife and fork pick off bite-sized portions of the chicken and add them to the soup.

8. Ladle the soup into bowls and allow each person to add their own seasoning of salt and black pepper, or just salt, if preferred. We always leave seasoning to the very end – it's to give the simple, flavourful ingredients time to blend without any distractions.

9. If you like, you can garnish your soup with some chopped up seaweed sheet, finely sliced spring onion or even toasted pine nuts.

Destination:

Bukchon Hanok Village &
Korea Furniture Museum, Seoul

Home

집
Jib

A Korean time machine

There's a place in Seoul where you can step back 600 years in time to the fourteenth century. And it was here that I found myself with my dear friend, Kyung-sook Shin, walking along cobblestone alleyways and peering into windows of homes that were built during the early Joseon dynasty. Welcome to Bukchon Hanok Village, a historic neighbourhood filled with around 900 *hanok*, the original Korean house, made of wood, stone and paper. Today, some are still private homes, but many have been renovated and converted into guest houses, restaurants and galleries. No matter their function, all are protected under historic preservation laws. Now nestled into the modern part of Seoul, the Bukchon Hanok Village is an extraordinary snapshot of Korean history.

Situated between two palaces, the village was originally occupied by Joseon dynasty nobility and high-ranking officials who served the royal family. The area remained untouched until the 1930s, when new *hanok* were added. In the 1960s, when Seoul was racing to modernise, the village was going to be renovated and the historic homes relocated. Thankfully, locals petitioned the government to save the neighbourhood, and won.

We arrived in front of a perfectly preserved, gated *hanok* that belonged to a friend of Kyung-sook's who had asked us to tea. Kyung-sook had arranged this special invitation for me, and I was so grateful. From my very first trip to Korea, I have been touched by the generosity of my Korean friends, who are always thinking about how to provide me with an unforgettable experience.

Our host opened the heavy wooden door in the stone front wall, and we stepped into an enclosed courtyard filled with evergreen trees. (In the spring, krape myrtle, trumpet creepers, bamboo, peonies, pumpkin flowers and red roses are in bloom in the courtyard gardens of many village homes). A short stone walkway led us towards the entrance.

We took our shoes off; the house was toasty warm from the heated flooring. I felt like I had stepped into the hush of a monastery; all was pristine and serene. The rooms had shiny wooden floors and parchment sliding windows, but no furniture. Our host opened a high cabinet and removed a small mahogany table, along with pillows for us to sit on.

Outside it had started snowing, gently powdering the evergreen trees in the garden. The white sky through the windows was the most marvellous backdrop to the carved wooden roof and stone walls, which seemed as if they were in technicolour. Everything felt so calm, so mysterious and foreign to me. Our host gently placed a stone teapot and small white porcelain cups on the little table and served us in the traditional manner of a tea ceremony. The hot *saenggang-cha* was the perfect remedy for a cold winter day. Made from grated ginger root that's been soaked in honey, it slipped down my throat and warmed my insides. Equally as warming was the way my host made me feel right at home. I learned the Korean way is to make all guests feel like family.

As a self-confessed minimalist, I was deeply enamoured with the house and shared with my host a discussion I had been having with myself for over twenty years. I admitted I felt out of step with friends and fellow New Yorkers, whose apartments were filled with objects and furniture, as I love an empty room. I hardly had any furniture in my apartment and, like the Koreans, I kept everything inside the closets. Here in the *hanok* village, I felt more at ease than in many New York City apartments. I asked my host his opinion.

"Don't get furniture!" he said immediately. "The Korean way is to put everything in closets and that's why our rooms are so serene. We don't need clutter."

I was finally validated!

My first trip to the village was in winter and there were few people around, but I have returned during the summer, when it is packed with tourists, students, families and couples. I learned that a favourite pastime for locals is to rent *hanbok*, the traditional Korean national dress, and visit the *hanok* village (and other historic sites like the Deoksugung Palace) to experience what it was like for their ancestors. It's such a delightful sight to see everyone enjoying the past in the present. I think it enhances Koreans' special bond – *jeong* – and deepens this reverence for their ancestors, forging a strong sense of cultural identity. It's truly history coming alive.

Bukchon Hanok Village
Address: 37, Gyedong-gil, Jongno-gu, Seoul
Website: www.hanok.seoul.go.kr

Inside the *hanok*

Developed in the fourteenth century during the Joseon dynasty, *hanok* were built from the available, natural materials of earth, wood and rock. The foundations were made of stones, with a frame of wooden beams and red clay tiled roofs. The size of the *hanok* depended on your social status, with the nobility living inside an estate with multiple structures.

Doors and windows were constructed from wooden lattices and panes made of parchment, not glass. This parchment, known as *hanji*, is made from the inner bark of the mulberry tree, and works perfectly to both insulate and ventilate the home.

Red clay, which ingeniously absorbs and regulates humidity, was used to finish the walls and floors. *Hanok* are kept warm in winter using *ondol*, an ancient underfloor heating system. A wood burning furnace in a lower kitchen sends heat upwards through channels under the stone floor.

Typically, *hanok* were built on sites facing a river with a mountain at the rear. The roofs have deep eaves to keep them shaded in the hot summer months. Further north, *hanok* were built in a closed square around a courtyard to keep it warm.

The houses were designed to incorporate both the Confucian ideal of living in harmony with nature and the practice of *Pungsu-jiri* (similar to Chinese Feng Shui), which focused on building your home in alignment with the environment for prosperity and luck. Because Confucian principles dictated separating the sexes, women lived in the interior quarters, and men in the exterior.

What I love about the *hanok* is how it all centres around nature. The houses were built with large picture windows facing courtyards, which were filled with trees and flowers. As Koreans sit on the floor, the windows were built low so they could put their elbow on a sill, look out and appreciate the vista. Koreans viewed everything outside their window as the garden, to be respected and enjoyed. There is a wonderful meditative quality to living like this – bringing nature into your everyday life is a key to achieving peace of mind.

What is interesting is that while *hanok* were once considered old-fashioned and not built to keep up with modern technology, today they are being celebrated for their eco-friendly, sustainable characteristices. As they were assembled pillar by pillar, tile by tile, they can be disassembled and rebuilt in a new location, making them truly portable architecture. Younger generations are now either buying *hanok* and refurbishing the interiors, or building new homes using old principles.

Modern living

If you want to understand how Koreans live today, you can think of it as a mathematical equation:

Ancient Confucian values + 21st-century architecture = home

Today, around 80 per cent of Korean's 51 million people are living in cities and urban areas, with about 10 million within Seoul.

Roughly 70 per cent of Korea is mountainous, making space a premium, and therefore since the 1960s, the country has been building vertically at a brisk pace. So while people do live in houses or villas (normally four storeys housing eight to ten apartments), the majority of Koreans today live in high-rise apartment complexes. With up to twenty buildings per complex, they can resemble a small village. Average prices for an apartment in Seoul range from US$350,000 to US$1.5 million.

(If luxury is what you are looking for, head to the Gangnam neighbourhood in Seoul. Home to K-pop stars, actors and tycoons, apartment living here is the height of opulence, with buildings often containing a spa, gym, pool and parking. The price of an apartment starts at around US$1.5 million and then heads up into the stratosphere.)

Each typical apartment, "*apatu*", has two or three bedrooms, a kitchen, living room, bathroom and utility room, along with large verandas used for storing food or drying laundry. Everyone I know in Seoul lives in modern, high-rise buildings, but there are some really exciting new living spaces appearing too, like warehouses being converted into cool apartments and shops.

From the outside, those high-rise apartments might be made of glass and steel but features of traditional *hanok* can still be found inside. Just like a *hanok*, a 21st-century apartment has a sunken entrance before you step into the rest of the space. In a *hanok* it was designed to capture rainwater; today, it is to remove and store your shoes. Korean apartments all have sliding, floor-length glass windows and doors, a feature that was common in a *hanok* home, though of course those walls and windows were made of paper. The underfloor heating system is also similar except that instead of wood smoke, contemporary homes use gas or electric heating pipes – much safer!

Floor culture

As I have already mentioned, the first, most important thing to know about visiting someone at home is that you must remove your shoes. There will be a space at the entrance to store them, and you may be given slippers or socks while you are visiting. For centuries, Koreans sat and slept on the floor (though many now live in a more Western fashion), so clean floors were, and still are, a must. Also, remember to bring a gift (see Chapter 1) to thank your host for the invitation.

Since I was a child, I've always preferred sitting on the floor to a sofa or chair – I think I was an early "listen to your body" kind of person. So I was enthralled to find myself among people who sit on the floor and don't wear shoes, and this is perhaps another reason why I felt so instantly at home in Korea.

There are so many physical health benefits to sitting on the floor. It improves your core strength, your hips, back posture and overall longevity. I still watch TV and read while sitting on the floor – I would recommend doing the same: start with just five, ten minutes at a time. Your body will be working without you even knowing it.

Getting up from the floor is a great exercise as well. Standing up from a seated position without using your hands and arms for support will not only strengthen your core muscles but improve your balance.

Hidden furniture

You might be surprised going into a Korean home because furnishings can be quite minimal. The first time I went into a traditional home I laughed to myself, as all the furniture was hidden in a closet and only taken out as needed. As I've said, for years I had been having arguments with myself about how much furniture I needed to live with. Friends urged me to furnish my home, but I prefer an empty room.

This is not to say Koreans have never lived with elaborate furnishings. To get a flavour for this, you must make a trip to the Korea Furniture Museum in Seoul. Opened in 1993, this private museum showcases the collection of Chyung Mi-Sook's 2500 pieces of antique Korean furniture and housewares from the Joseon era (1392–1910).

I was so lucky to hear about the Furniture Museum, a hidden gem that is not on the tourist map, which must be booked in advance through its website. Anton Hur, an award-winning translator, urged me to go, promising it would be worth the trip. I took a taxi up a winding road in the middle of what looked like a forest to the village of Seongbuk-gu, north of Seoul. The museum is situated behind a stone wall, and it's only after you enter through the gate that you learn that the collection is distributed throughout ten *hanok* and a palatial main building, in a village setting designed to depict the way the Korean nobility lived during the Joseon dynasty.

I wandered through bedrooms, sitting rooms, kitchens and women's and men's quarters. There were eighteenth- and nineteenth-century, late-Joseon-dynasty bookcases, small dining tables and chests, some with mother-of-pearl inlay, all carved to highlight the grain of the wood. Desks were built lower to the ground to accommodate the tradition of sitting on the floor and designed to complement the size of the windows. Ornate screens were adorned with intricate patterns of the Korean motifs of birds and flowers.

Don't leave before walking through the stone Bullomun Gate, "the gate of eternal life", situated in the middle of the grounds. They say those who step though it will turn ten years younger.

Is there a more perfect function for a gate?

Korea Furniture Museum
Address: 121 Daesagwan-ro, Seongbuk-gu, Seoul
Website: www.kofum.com

Young love

Korean life is very much centred around the family (more on this in Chapter 4); young people tend to live at home with their parents rather than move into university dorms or apartments, which makes privacy a thorny issue, particularly when it comes to dating. How can young adults get intimate when their parents are right there in the house watching TV?

Well, to every problem there is a solution!

Welcome to the world of "love hotels", which are unique to Korea. These hotels often have themed rooms, for example a spa, hip-hop or game room, and can be rented overnight or for a number of hours. Some love hotels offer a choice of Korean-style rooms with a mat and blankets or Western-style rooms with a bed. Many have very colourful, cartoon-like décor – you can sleep in a gigantic glass slipper or in a box of French fries!

These love hotels can be found all over Korea, often in busy neighbour-hoods where there is a lot of nightlife. To keep everything private, couples can either book a room online or pay through an electronic kiosk at the entrance. Their parents will never know!

Lessons from a Korean home

• Make a practice of sitting on the floor. It will build your core and make you feel strong!

• Free your feet. Always remove your shoes when in your home or visiting others. You don't need to bring the outside dirt in.

• Less is more. Clear the clutter to create tranquillity in your home.

• Open your windows all year round – fresh air is rejuvenating.

• If you live in an apartment, bring the outside inside with flowers and plants. Studies have shown plants act as air filters and can improve your mood.

• On your walls, frame photographs or posters of nature to add serenity to a room.

• Focus on having natural materials like wood and ceramic in your home. These sustainable materials bring us in harmony with nature.

• Enjoy tea by making a little ceremony out of it, even if it's just for yourself. Use a special teapot and cup. Savour don't gulp!

계란 간장
밥

(Gyeran gan
jangbap)

This recipe comes from my friend, Won-pyun Sohn, author of *Almond*. Won-pyun used to cook a lot but confesses she has now shifted her efforts to more simple fare, like this dish.

"Egg soy sauce rice is a popular, delectable and easy-to-make Korean dish that doesn't require any special ingredients and can be cooked by anyone. So this is the perfect recipe for those who want to try their hands at homemade Korean food, especially first-timers.

"A humble dish, it is nothing more than a bowl of steamed rice seasoned with soy sauce and sesame oil, with a sunny-side-up or scrambled egg on top. But that's also why it has such a special place in my heart."

Ingredients

(Serves 1)

200g rice
2 tbsp soy sauce
1 tbsp sesame oil
2 eggs

1. Prepare 200g of steamed rice according to the packet instructions. Put it in a bowl and stir in the soy sauce and sesame oil, ensuring all the grains get a good coating. (If you're partial to spicy foods, you can add a tablespoon of red pepper paste as well.)

2. Now prepare your favourite kind of cooked egg: it could be fried, sunny side up, or scrambled, or any other way you like.

3. Place the cooked egg on top of the rice. If you add some cooked vegetables to this dish, you can turn it into a *bibimbap*. Consider egg soy sauce rice as a sort of minimalist *bibimbap*.

Destination:
DMZ

Family

가족
Gajok

The great divide

Can you imagine being separated from your child for more than half a century? Or having your mother or brother, father, grandparents or best friend ripped from your arms – never to see them again?

Well, that's what happened and is happening today at the DMZ, the Demilitarised Zone, the border of North and South Korea. It's a living reminder of the disaster of the Korean War and the continuing friction between the two sides.

A quick but important history lesson: Korea began as one country under the Joseon dynasty from 1392 to 1910, when it was annexed by Japan. At the end of World War II, following the surrender of the Japanese troops,

Korea was partitioned by the Allied Powers. The Soviet Union occupied the North and the US occupied the South. It was the opposing ideologies of these two superpowers that provided the basis of hostility between North and South. Tensions escalated and led to the outbreak of the Korean War (1950–1953), which ended in a stalemate.

The DMZ was established in 1953 under the terms of the armistice agreement that ended the war. It is a 160-mile long, 2.5-mile-wide border made up of high barbed-wire fences and watchtowers manned by armed soldiers. Over the years there have been occasional incidents and skirmishes between the two sides, some of them quite serious.

The physical proximity between these two dramatically contrasting worlds of North and South is mind-boggling. The DMZ is only about 30 miles from the centre of Seoul, where anyone has the freedom to listen to K-pop boy band sensation BTS, wear jeans and use the internet. While just over the border, millions of their fellow countrymen are starving and are essentially slaves to their totalitarian leader. This stark difference between freedom and bondage is palpable – it pulsates in the air and across the landscape.

To truly understand Korea, you must see the DMZ, because the trauma and pain of the Korean War and the separation between the North and South reverberates still in every family, in films, TV and literature. Author Won-pyun Sohn, told me the protagonist of her book, *Almond*, was based on her own grandmother, who walked from the North to the South after the war carrying her mother in her arms.

The separation of the country is so complicated and painful that today many Koreans say it's too "difficult" to talk about. The younger generation of South Koreans have little attachment to the North, and the dream of a unified Korea is becoming more and more distant. It is a searing example of *han*, the Korean philosophy of grit and endurance born out of the despair and pain of generations of families torn apart.

For nearly 70 years, South Korean brothers and sisters, mothers and fathers, sons and daughters have placed banners and tokens of hope and peace on the fence at the Freedom Bridge (connecting North and South Korea for prisoner exchanges, and now closed) to send messages of love to their families separated by war.

A disaster tourist

To visit the DMZ, you must go with an approved tour company and bring your passport and identifying documents.

It was a freezing January morning ten years ago when I visited the DMZ for the first time. There were hardly any visitors – only me and four Japanese tourists. We travelled on a bus from Seoul before being transferred to a military bus when we got near the North/South divide. On board, we were given an extremely stern lecture and instructions about our visit. No cameras whatsoever – the North Korean soldiers could and would shoot us if they saw us taking photographs of them. We were warned about making arm and hand gestures towards the Northern border – inches away from where we would be. We could be shot and killed if a North Korean soldier saw a gesture from anyone – it had happened before.

We learned about the murder of two US Soldiers in 1976, a cautionary tale that anything can flare up in the DMZ. After a peace summit between the North and South, a pine tree was planted. A few days later, two US soldiers were trimming the branches that blocked the view from one of the offices. Out of nowhere, two North Korean soldiers approached and murdered them with axes, an incident that nearly started another war. Thankfully, it was averted. But the DMZ is a dangerous place where anything can happen.

As we approached, I saw soldiers in formation dotted around the grounds with guns and tanks. I had never been to an active warzone in my life and it was quite shocking.

So, with trepidation but also a sense of adventure and daring, I walked off the bus and into the Joint Security Area. It is the only place you can freely step into North Korea, via a small negotiating room that is part of the complex in the former village of Panmunjom. It's comprised of several bright-blue buildings that resemble pieces on a Monopoly board.

The building that contains the central conference room where peace talks have been held is open to the public. Inside is a wooden table with a South Korean soldier stationed on one end, a North Korean at the other. The border actually runs down the centre of the table, so when you walk around the table on the north side, you essentially cross into North Korea.

The Northern soldier stood so rigid he reminded me of the gigantic machine-gun-toting doll in *Squid Game*. I felt like I was in a Hollywood movie and the negotiating room was a film set.

It was a sombre visit. I walked to the Freedom Bridge, which crosses the Imjin River, connecting South to North, and saw the banners, letters, mementos and gifts pinned to the barbed-wire fence. I read the letters and looked at the old, yellowed photos left by South Koreans praying for their families living in the North. You can feel the pain of families and friends who have been separated.

A few years later, I had the honour of representing *The Accusation,* by a North Korean writer using the pseudonym Bandi, which had been heroically smuggled out of the North.

The book's collection of stories depicts the everyday lives of North Korean families. It is heart-breaking in its evocation of their suffering under the totalitarian regime. *The Accusation* was published in more than fifteen countries, and I felt the best way to honour Bandi's work was to bring foreign publishers to the DMZ and read from the book, sending a message of hope across the border.

On a beautiful autumn day, this dream was realised. The fifteen international publishers and I gathered on Freedom Bridge and read from the book in Swedish, Dutch, Finnish, Italian, English, Spanish, French, Russian, Danish, Korean, Catalan, Norwegian, Slovenian, Persian, German, Czech, Chinese, Indonesian, Portugese, Romanian, Hungarian and Polish. We held each other and the tears flowed. Our voices became an operatic chorus, singing for freedom.

Since 1985, some 44,000 families have been allowed to reunite, thanks to family reunion programmes. Family members are chosen by lottery, and for them it must feel like winning billions. The last time a reunion lottery was held was in 2018, when 89 South Koreans and 83 North Koreans met with family members over three days. Photos and gifts were exchanged, along with tears and the painful understanding that they were not likely to meet again.

DMZ as Disneyland

Today you can find rides, games, restaurants and shops at the DMZ, as it has become a tourist hotspot, with 1.2 million visitors annually. Along with the Freedom Bridge, you can visit the Dorasan Peace Park, dedicated to reunification, and the Dora Observatory, where you can use telescopes to see across to North Korea. You can also take a Peace Gondola ride across the Imjin River for a bird's-eye view of the demarcation line or walk along the Infiltration Tunnel built by the North to spy on the South. The tunnel was only discovered in the 1970s after a North Korean defector reported its existence, only two kilometres from the Joint Security Base at Panmunjon.

I donned a hardhat and walked down a steep ramp into the tunnel, built 155 feet below the earth. Climbing back up is a lot harder than going down! The tunnel is large enough for tanks and military vehicles. Walking into its depths, I could easily envision an invasion. The air was very cold, and anxiety reared inside me, along with my occasional claustrophia. I seemed to be walking for ever, until, eventually, I came to the end of the tunnel, cemented and blocked off from North Korea. I placed my hand on the rock-hard wall, unnerved that only a few feet away was the North.

Then, to my astonishment, I saw a small water fountain with a sign inviting visitors to drink. Called *manghangsu* "water of nostalgia", the fountain water is said to soothe the grief of those who come to see their homeland divided. The water comes from an underground spring, completely unpolluted by man. I drank it. I can taste it now in my memory, so cold and pure.

Initially, I found the idea of the DMZ as a tourist attraction a bit strange. But as I travelled back to Seoul on the military bus, I thought about the possibilities of the DMZ. If there is peace or reunification one day, we would be able to witness what has become of the untouched area of land within the zone. With its flora and fauna left alone for decades, it has ironically become a Garden of Eden (see Chapter 5).

Now I think a visit is an important opportunity to learn about the Korean War and reflect on the tragedy of the situation. Maybe the commercialisation of the DMZ will de-escalate hostilities and bring the two countries together to finally sign a peace treaty and end the Korean War. It's a beginning. Today, I see this as a very positive sign.

Korean family values

The most important thing to Koreans is family, which for them includes both their relatives and their fellow countrymen, whom they see as extended family. This belief is deeply rooted in the teachings of Confucius (sixth century BC) who taught that if the nuclear family was strong and happy, so too was the country. So family harmony was, and is, all.

Confucian tradition dictated that in Korean families, the father was the head of the household, and he made all decisions for the family. Reverence for elders was paramount. Men and women had defined roles – mothers took care of children and the home, fathers worked outside in the fields. Sons stayed with their families when they married, while daughters went to live with their in-laws (this must have been the cause of much friction in past centuries too!) The eldest son was responsible for caring for his parents in their old age, mourning them ritually after death and inheriting the wealth and leadership of the family.

21st-century families

The rugged individualism so prized in some Western cultures has no place in 21st-century Korean life. Instead, Korean families continue to practise the Confucian teachings of family interdependence, duty and respect for elders, with some adjustments for modern life.

Today, elders and ancestors are still treasured. It is considered disgraceful to treat older people or one's grandparents poorly. When dining with the family and guests, the grandparents and oldest person at the table begin eating first. Ancestors receive the same reverence at ancestral rite ceremonies, *jesa*, which are held on anniversaries and major holidays like Lunar New Year. To honour them, a feast is prepared, incense is lit and prayers are offered.

Curiously, with people's busy lives, it has become a custom for families to pay Buddhist monks to create ancestral banquets in temples and pray for their ancestors on their behalf. (Professional mourners are a common practice in Korea and elsewhere in Asia.)

Today, even though most Koreans live in modern cities, where possible, in-laws still reside with their married children and grandchildren. (In America, this arrangement would be turned into a sitcom. In Korea, it is the subject of a number of K-dramas.) The women in the home are carers for their elders – parents and grandparents are rarely placed in nursing homes.

Education is priority numer one in Korean family life for adults and children. I think the education of children and the value placed on books, poetry, debate and discussion is one reason why Korea has developed so rapidly in the last few decades.

While arranged marriages were once the norm, love marriages are starting to become more common, although family input is still important. They say in Korea, a marriage is not just about the couple, but a union of families, and as such, it's best if everyone's values align.

Young Koreans do, however, take their time dating. First, there is a period of becoming friends and getting to know one another, then they may officially begin a relationship. To me, this feels like a smart way of doing things. In our fast-paced world driven by the internet and social media, people think they know each other by a tweet or post... but not so.

In the West, couples mark anniversaries by the year, in Korea, couples celebrate every 100 days. The number is significant in Korean culture; it means happy and fulfilled. So the 100th day of dating is considered your first anniversary, and rings are exchanged.

Once married, husbands and wives are more equal in decision making than in previous generations. The idea that only men can run the family is no longer the rule. One thing you won't find in Korea are multitudes of nurseries and day care centres – grandparents take care of their grandchildren.

I have found that many young people live at home with their parents until they are married, or at least 25. This is so different from life in the West, where children leave home at eighteen to study or become independent of their families. In Korea, parental involvement in their children's lives and futures is intense, and children want to please and honour their parents.

What is so interesting about Korean life is that family and home are synonymous. When children do eventually fly the nest to marry or work, the place where they have grown up is still considered their "home". Since family home is always inherited by the eldest son and does not leave the family (much like the English practice of primogeniture), it means that children, grandchildren and relatives always have a home to call their own.

Remember the last time you applied for a job? Your prior work experience and success in your role would have been the most important information to convey. In Korea, the most important thing on your resumé is… your family. On all applications for university/school and jobs, the first questions asked are: "Who is your father, your mother? What do they do? Where is your family home? "

Questions about your family come first. This, of course, brings its own issues. Orphans, for instance, may lose out on opportunities because they can't provide their family background.

We are one

Koreans are unusual in that they see their fellow countrymen as extended family. Perhaps because they were enslaved and attacked by the Chinese and Japanese for centuries, suffered deprivation and loss of relatives in wars, each child is precious, and friends and neighbours are valued as family. They had to rely on each other for survival then; today, their "nation of families" philosophy has allowed Koreans to thrive in terms of their cultural and economic place in the world.

A lesson in *jeong*: gold patriots

In 1997, the Asian financial crisis arrived on Korea's doorstep, nearly bankrupting the country. The International Monetary Fund came to the rescue with a bailout loan of US$58 billion. (Alongside conditions that included austerity and banking reforms.) What followed was the ultimate lesson in *jeong*.

In 1998, the government called on every Korean to sell (below market prices) or donate gold to help pay back the loan. They called their campaign "Collect gold for the love of Korea".

Gold is very important in Korean culture; it is used as gifts for milestones like birthdays, weddings or retirement. But soon after the call went out, 3.5 million Koreans sold and donated their gold for the country: athletes donated medals, families donated wedding rings, and businesses their gold "luck" keys. Cardinal Kim, the former Archbishop of Seoul, donated his gold cross.

Overall, Koreans donated US$2.2 billion in gold, all of which was melted into ingots and used to pay off a portion of the debt. They worked together as one big family to save the economy, sacrificing their own personal savings for the future of their country.

Family ties

The Korean focus on family can also be very complicated and a source of pain for those who do not come from a traditional family structure. Because of the Confucian stress on ancestral bloodlines, adoption in Korea is rarely practised. I have heard of Korean parents who have adopted in secret because of the social taboo.

After the Korean War, many orphaned and abandoned babies were adopted by families in the US and Europe. But in 2011, the law was changed to slow foreign adoptions and boost domestic ones, keeping Korean children within their culture.

Korea was embarrassed to be such a wealthy country that appeared to be exporting its babies. Yet the reluctance to adopt and the brakes on inter-country adoptions means orphanages are brimming with Korean babies the Koreans don't want.

Today there is a push to encourage adoption and reduce the stigma un-married mothers face about raising children.

Another complex issue in Korea is sexual orientation. When it comes to the LGBTQ community, Korea is way behind other countries and still very conservative. I have seen the lengths that some young adults and children go to in order to hide their sexual orientation from their parents and society. I wonder if this stems from a desire by parents for their children to replicate the traditional family, because once this was their means of survival. People have to live in hiding for fear of being ostracised, estranged from their families and having their lives ruined.

There is no same sex marriage in Korea, and while gay people can serve in the military (transgender individuals cannot), reports suggest they endure much discrimination and bullying. Until April 2022, the courts upheld im-prisonment for soldiers who engaged in gay sex however, the Supreme Court of Korea recently ruled that sex between soldiers away from military bases cannot be prosecuted. This is a big step forward for gay rights in Korea.

Even though Korean courts don't recognise married same sex couples, I have gay friends who are married and there is a growing community of sup-port for them. More gay and lesbian Koreans are coming out of the closet, but most keep their orientation a secret from their families and co-work-ers, even as younger generations become more tolerant. Further progress was made in 2022 when LGBTQ candidates ran in local Korean elections, aiming to increase visibility for the community and participate in making policy.

Ironically, heterosexuals will often hold hands with friends of the same gender and display affection towards each other publicly. When Kyung-sook

Shin and I travel together or just go for a stroll in Seoul, she always takes my hand and we walk arm-in-arm. It's a lovely tradition that I have only encountered in Korea.

The cities of Seoul, Busan and Daegu all have gay neighbourboods with clubs and bars, but they keep a low profile. Ask your Korean friends for suggestions. There is a Queer Culture Festival and several travel agencies that specialise in gay travel which I'd advise you to contact if you want to enjoy the gay scene. (Gay and lesbian tourists in Korea who are open about their sexuality should expect some shocked and even hostile reactions from locals.)

I'm thrilled that in the world of literature, LGBTQ books and authors are often the most sought after. *Love In the Big City*, by Sang Young Park (translated by Anton Hur), a story about a young gay man searching for happiness in Seoul became a bona fide international bestseller. *Violets*, by Kyung-sook Shin, tells the story of a young woman whose life crumbles after she is spurned by her young female lover. The book garnered some of the best critical reviews of the author's career in the US and UK and is being reissued in Korea.

Korea has a long way to go in terms of gay rights and acceptance but I think its literature is leading the way.

Lessons from family

- Cherish your family bonds (yes, even your in-laws!) – they are your foundation and security. And when I say family, I refer to both biological and the ones that we create with our friends. Deep connections will make us stronger and more successful.

- Honour and nurture your elders, and understand it is your duty to take care of them when needed. Adopt an older friend! Having friends of all ages will make you more balanced, empathetic, smarter and happier.
- Your countrymen are your extended family. You only succeed when you succeed together. Get out of your comfort zone to help someone or meet someone new.
- Put down your phones, turn off your TVs and invite a friend or neighbour to share a meal.
- To have good friends, be a good friend. Learn from the sacrifice and dedication of Koreans and incorporate these traits into your everyday relationships. We must not allow ourselves to become isolated and self-absorbed.

Red Algae Cold Noodles

우무국

(Woomoogook)

This is a "spoken recipe" recorded by Ha Mi-hyun – a woman on a mission. After an extended stay at a temple in Mungyeong, Ha Mi-hyun, who grew up in Busan, became obsessed with the flavours and health benefits of temple food. She discovered that the recipes had been handed down for generations among monks, farmers and villagers, but never recorded.

Leaving the temple, Ha resolved to gather these local "spoken recipes", so they could take their rightful place in Korean cuisine. She founded the Spoken Company, dedicated to preserving and sharing these unique regional dishes. So far she has done field research in over 70 regions in Korea, and recorded more than 400 recipes, now collected into a book. I love that Ha describes her job as a "mouth-to-mouth foodist".

Ingredients

(Serves 1)

150g dried red algae
(agar-agar weed)

Broth

1 tbsp barley flour*
½ tbsp soy sauce
150ml cold water
* If you can't find
barley flour, use 150ml
almond or oat milk
instead of the broth.

Garnish

10g chives, chopped
1 tsp vinegar
Cane sugar (or brown
sugar)

1. Boil the dried red algae in a large saucepan of water for an hour.

2. Set a sieve or colander over a large bowl and gently pour the whole saucepan of algae and water into it. You'll be using the water and disposing of the red algae.

3. Leave the algae water for an hour at room temperature until it becomes a gelatinous block.

4. Slice the block into noodle-shaped strips.

5. In a bowl, stir the barley flour and soy sauce into the 150ml cold water. This will be the broth. (Alternatively use almond or oat milk.)

6. Make a bed of noodle strips in the broth and garnish the dish with the chopped-up chives.

7. Season the noodles with vinegar, sugar and other spices as you wish.

Destination:

Seoraksan National Park & Museum SAN, Wonju

Nature

자연

Jayeon

Three for the road

I am very lucky to have Korean friends who share my sense of adventure: the author, Kyung-sook Shin, agent, Joseph Lee, and I have become the Three Musketeers when it comes to travel. They have taken me to so many incredible places and are always eager to join me for more. When I heard about the Museum SAN (meaning "mountain", as well as being an acronym for Space Art Nature), a museum devoted to nature, two hours' drive south-west from Seoul in the mountains of Wonju, I called my fellow musketeers saying we had to visit and – *voilà* – we were on the road!

It was winter and the mountains were brown but snow-capped. As usual, the sky was what I call Korean blue – think bright technicolour. Driving for hours with wonderful friends who are interesting conversationalists makes every trip the best in the world. When we eventually approached our destination, I saw a monumental structure of glass and concrete perched on a mountaintop in Wonju's Oak Valley.

Designed by famed Japanese architect Tadao Ando, the building is stark and lean, and blends into the landscape. "I wanted to create a garden museum in the sky, a dreamlike museum like no other," he has said. And that is the point of the museum: to celebrate, absorb, meditate and become one with nature. The motto of the museum is "disconnect to connect" and it couldn't be more apt.

A water garden surrounds the museum, reflecting the landscape and flower beds. I could only imagine how colourful it would be in the summer when everything would be in bloom.

As we meandered along the walkways in the Stone Garden, we were accompanied by the sounds of tiny birds chirping and, through the trees, soft Buddhist chanting. The garden contains nine stone mounds inspired by the tombs of the Silla kingdom (57 BC – 935 CE). They seemed like gentle waves in the ocean and reminded me of the sculptures of Maya Lin. The mounds were lightly dusted with snow, and the three of us placed our palms on them, leaving our handprints there.

A real highlight was James Turrell's permanent exhibition of light and space. Like the late conceptual artist Christo (who wrapped buildings and islands in fabric), James Turrell is an artist who transforms the earth itself and shows us nature as we have never seen it before. At SAN, Turrell has built rooms of different shapes and sizes with changing light and colour. It is a completely transformative experience; light shifts and bounces, making you feel as if you are walking up a staircase or towards the end of a wall, only to find you are stepping onto a terrace that overlooks the entire valley!

When I visited, the Meditation Hall was not yet completed, but it is on my list for my next trip. It is built as a cocoon of serenity and silence where visitors can meditate and truly disconnect to connect.

Museum SAN
Address: 260 Oakvalley 2-gil, Jijeong-myeon, Wonju-si, Gangwon-do
Website: www.museumsan.org

Perfect harmony

On a visit to the in the Seoul Museum of Art, I became mesmerised by an ancient ceramic moon jar. It looked so natural, as if it had sprouted from a seed. The jar, a perfect sphere, so smooth and round, bore a tiny indentation on the lip. A mistake?

"Imperfection is perfection. It was crafted that way intentionally," my Korean friend said.

In Korea, natural beauty is the highest order of beauty. People cherish nature in all its variations, from the *han* of a storm to the *heung* of cherry blossom season. Everywhere you go, you see and feel their reverence for the natural world.

The majority of the land in Korea is mountainous, so it's no surprise hiking is their national pastime. *Heung*, joy, is to be found walking in the mountains. While the Japanese may curb nature with bonsai and the Chinese prefer to enclose it within high walls, the Korean philosophy is to live in harmony with it. All Korean gardens focus on natural beauty. To deviate from nature is to dishonour it. A garden's affinity with its surroundings, with water, wood and stone, is its guiding principle.

Pack your lunch and hit the trail

Koreans love to hike, and one thing that surprises tourists is how seriously they take this pursuit. No basic shorts and sneakers here! Two out of every three Koreans own hiking boots. They like to wear mountaineering clothes, both on and off the mountain. If you join a Korean group of hikers, also know you will be eating along the route, and I am not talking about fruits or nuts. Hikers bring a full meal and, to wash it down, rice wine; as is the Korean way, everything is shared.

Koreans have always had a special relationship with the mountains and forests that surround them. In ancient times, they believed mountains had their own spirits and life force – *gi* – and going into the mountains would improve your own *gi* (which modern science has proven is correct.)

When Korea began to modernise in the 1960s and many moved from the countryside to cities, the government promoted hiking as a form of team building among co-workers. This kicked off what has today become everyone's favourite weekend sport.

My associate agent, Sue Park, used to go hiking a lot with her family when she was small. She believes it's become popular among families because it gives them quality time together in nature.

"Mountains have always been considered a place for meditation and sublimity in Korean culture; they're supposed to help you find your inner balance, attune your mind to the natural order, and even cleanse you spiritually," she told me. "Hence so many Asian ink paintings of famous mountains, including Mount Geumgangsan, Baekdu Mountain and the Kumgang Mountains." (The latter two have always been considered emblems of sublimity in Korean culture, and in ancient times Koreans believed that *shinsuns*, god-like Taoist hermits, resided there.)

"My family also made a pretty big deal out of procuring drinking water from these hiking trips. Some Korean mountains have extremely well-known mineral springs – where you have to wait in lines for your turn. Many people fill up huge water canisters (ones that Americans might think are for gasoline), which they will take home."

Hiking is popular in all strata of Korean society, even the very top. In 2018, South Korean President Moon Jae-in and Northern leader Kim Jong-un met for a rare summit, after which they climbed Mount Paektu from the North Korean side together. President Moon is an avid hiker and climber and has trekked in the Himalayas, but this climb made history.

Climbing the mountain

With 22 national parks in Korea, beautiful mountain trails await you in every direction. One of the most popular is the Seoraksan National Park, which is three hours by car from Seoul. Famous for its Buddhist temples, 2000 animal species, 1400 rare plants species, pine forests and 30 mountain peaks, the park was designated a Biosphere Preservation District by UNESCO.

In Korea, people typically hike with friends, family or hiking clubs. You can also book and join a tour if you are travelling solo. Mount Seoraksan is the highest peak (1708 metres/5603 feet), but there are many trails for varying abilities which begin at the park entrance, where you can get a map and choose your route. (There is also a cable car for those who want to enjoy the view but are unable to hike.)

Fringe benefits

Koreans hike because it gives them time to connect with family while de-stressing from often intense work and school schedules. Of course, hiking has many other benefits, such as increased heart and muscle strength – all those hills and rocks! Research has also shown that being in nature boosts your creativity and ability to problem-solve. One study by researchers at the University of California, Berkeley, even found that experiencing the beauty of the outdoors makes us more trusting and generous, because it increases positive emotions.

Author You-jeong Jeong says she hikes to clear and reset her mind and body. "I go hiking mostly when my mind is in turmoil or when I feel burnt out, to awaken my body through extreme exercise."

Reclaim and restore

One thing that made a lasting impression on me in Korea is the effort the country has made to transform urban spaces into green havens, allowing Koreans to find a calm refuge outside their front doors.

Seoul Forest Park, which has been compared to Hyde Park in London and Central Park in New York City, has had many incarnations: as a water treatment facility, a racetrack, a golf course and a sports park. After a major rebuilding effort, it opened in 2005 as a public park that includes natural wildlife habitats, an eco-forest and a butterfly garden. It is now filled with locals picnicking, while enjoying the cherry blossoms in spring and the golde gingko trees in autumn.

Another green development in 2005 was the US$380 million urban renewal of nearly 6 kilometres of the Cheonggyecheon stream that runs through downtown Seoul. After the Korean War, the stream had been paved over with concrete and later built up with elevated highways. Both were removed so the stream would flow once more, while green walkways were created. Today, thousands of people flock daily to what is considered the green heart of Seoul, allowing them to decompress in nature while in the middle of a busy city.

The Korean Garden of Eden

The DMZ (as I mentioned in Chapter 4) is the only place on earth that has had a 70-year respite from humans – no one has walked on it, developed it, paved it, or destroyed its trees and wildlife, or polluted its water. Rather ironically, it has become a Garden of Eden, an untouched ecosystem where plants and animals have flourished without intervention. It is now home to more than 5000 species, 106 of which have protected status.

In 2018, North Korean leader Kim Jong-un and South Korean President Moon Jae-in pledged to "transform the demilitarised zone into a peace zone in a genuine sense" by ending all hostile acts along the border. One year later, South Korea opened the first of three "peace trails" for a limited number of visitors along the DMZ. Through nature, maybe families will finally be reunited. That would be so Korean!

Discover the walk here: www.dmzwalk.com

Island mystery

The sea around the South Korean peninsula is peppered with over 3350 islands, many of them boasting spectacular landscapes and natural attractions. But there is one island that offers something beyond picture-perfect scenery: mystery.

Ulleungdo Island, 120 kilometres off the east coast of Korea, is a must for nature lovers with a thirst for adventure. It's a 2.5-hour train ride or 3-hour car ride, followed by a 3.5-hour ferry ride on choppy seas to get there. (Bring seasickness medicine with you.)

Due to its remoteness and inaccessibility, the island has been uninhabited for most of its history. And between 1400 and 1882, this was enforced by the Josean dynasty's "empty-island policy" out of fear of a Japanese invasion.

In the 1880s, Korea started to gradually repopulate the island.

The whole island is in fact a volcano covered in lush forests and waterfalls, with a dramatic coastline of volcanic rock and hiking trails. The surrounding waters are a marine protected area, so it's also a scuba diver's paradise.

Sounds mystical and other-worldly? Koreans think so, which is why they have nicknamed it "Mysterious Island". They believe that due to its pristine environment, in which fertile land meets clear, open skies, the island has a spiritual energy. Who doesn't want to soak that up?

Lessons from the natural world

- Go outdoors as much as you can. Soaking up nature improves your physical health, happiness and creativity.
- Make hiking a habit – to bond with family or friends and as an opportunity to clear your mind. Bring a delicious picnic as a reward for all your hard physical effort.
- Never tame nature – appreciate its wildness and beauty. Live in harmony with it.
- Explore new places outdoors where you live. Visit sculpture gardens, pick apples at an orchard, go whale watching or star gazing.

My friend and client J.M. Lee, author of *Broken Summer*, says this dish is more than a meal for him; it's a reminder of the beauty of the rainy season.

"Some dishes magically stir up happy memories from deep in our heart and bring them to the surface. The Korean spring onion pancake, to me, is a dish like that. Whenever raindrops start to fall, I feel an instant craving for this pancake, not unlike Pavlov's Dog, and cannot help fantasizing about its sweet fragrance and the crispy first bite.

"Raindrops drumming the roof and rainwater sloshing off the eaves all bring to mind a spring onion pancake sizzling in a frying pan – along with its irresistible aroma and taste. Unsurprisingly, the rainy season in Korea entices restaurant-goers out of other places into those selling spring onion pancakes.

"Humble as it might look, the spring onion pancake is incredibly versatile. It makes a healthy, easy-to-whip-up bite, and can be also served as a proper meal if you increase the ratio of flour. Flavour it with soy sauce or *chogochujang* (a mixture of *gochujang* – Korean chilli paste – and vinegar), and it will wonderfully complement any meal as a side dish. Its best friends are staple Korean drinks such as *makgeolli* (Korean rice wine) or *soju* (Korean hard liquor), but well-paired wine won't disappoint, either.

"My usual go-to toppings are strips of bacon or ham; a brilliant collaboration of East and West at the dining table. The bacon, needless to say, tastes marvellous, but the sizzling sound of it being pan-fried makes the whole experience even more exciting. In Korea, we're on the verge of this year's rainy season, yet again. And I'll be listening to the wonderful duet of the sound of rain outside my windows and the sweet spring onion pancake sizzling in an oiled pan."

Ingredients

(Makes 1 pancake)

5-10 small spring onions
* You could also add
some slivers of cabbage
and carrot
100g plain flour (if you
prefer a crispy texture,
you can replace half the
plain flour with tempu-
ra flour)
200ml water
2 eggs (1 for the batter,
and 1 for the topping)
Salt and black pepper
1-2 tbsps of cooking oil
of your choice

Topping(s)

Handful of mixed sea-
food, (oysters, mussels,
squid, prawns, or
clams), steamed for 2
mins, then pat dry with
a tea towel. (If using
squid, chop it into 1cm
x 1cm pieces)
3 strips of bacon, fried
(4–5 strips if you forego
the seafood)

Sauce

1 tbsp gochujang paste
1 tbsp vinegar

1. Wash the spring onions under running water and slice them in half lengthways and trim them so they are approximately 1–2cm shorter than the frying pan's diameter.* The shorter you cut them, the easier it'll be to flip the pancake later.

2. In a bowl, mix the flour, water and 1 egg, with some seasoning to create a batter. For a crispier pancake, use chilled water or 2–3 ice cubes instead. But take care not to add too many or the batter will be too watery.

3. Preheat your frying pan until smoking hot. Grease it with 1 tablespoon of cooking oil and turn the heat down to a medium setting.

4. Dip the spring onions into the batter, making sure they are thoroughly coated, and spread them out in the pan in a circular shape.

5. Pour the batter over the spring onions and tip the pan so it covers the base.

6. Sprinkle the seafood mix all over the pancake, as you would on a pizza.

7. Lay the strips of bacon over the seafood toppings.

8. Evenly spread the other egg – either straight from the shell or beaten – on the pancake and let it cook for 3–4 minutes.

9. Flip the pancake and use a spatula to press it down into the pan to help the ingredients stick together. Cook for a further 3 minutes or so, slipping 1–2 teaspoons of cooking oil around the edges so it won't stick.

10. Flip the pancake over to the topping side, and transfer to a plate and eat with the gochujang sauce (equal parts gochujang paste and vinegar combined).

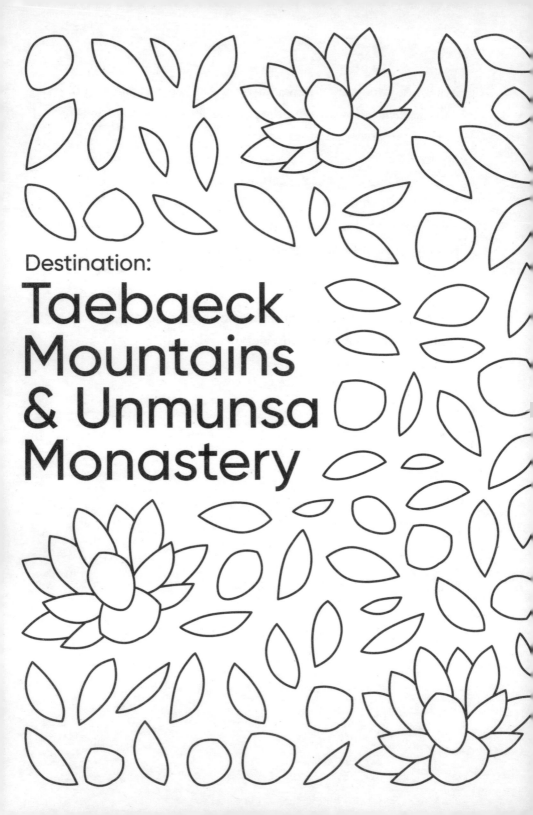

Destination:
Taebaeck Mountains & Unmunsa Monastery

Enlightenment

계몽

Gyemong

The land of the morning calm

Korea was once known as the kingdom of Chosun, which loosely translates as "The land of the morning calm". (American businessman Percival Lowell travelled through Korea in the 1880s and wrote the book, *Choson, The Land of the Morning Calm: A Sketch of Korea*, popularising the phrase outside of the country.)

With its beautiful mountain ranges, tranquil lakes, lush green forests and gentle mornings, there really is no better description. I think the phrase also speaks to the practice of Korean Buddhism, which advocates the pursuit of mindfulness and compassion through daily Zen meditation.

Buddhism has been a part of Korean life since the fourth century, when it arrived via China. Today, about one quarter of Koreans identify as Buddhist, and there are a total of around 20,000 temples in the country. Of these, only about 900 are considered "traditional". (To register as "traditional", a Buddhist temple must satisfy a set of criteria: religious integrity, architectural and historical value, and ownership. Temples not registered as "traditional" are those managed by individual monks following different, newer doctrines, or even private properties run by individuals.)

While they can be found all over the country, many are in mountain valleys, perfect spots to focus and pray without distraction. In Korea, everyone is welcome to visit any temple, but if you want to have the full experience with the space and time to emotionally recharge, you can stay in one as a guest through the organisation Templestay. Created by the Korean Cultural Organisation for tourists coming to the 2002 World Cup to experience Korean Buddhism and culture, more than 50 temples now welcome you for stays lasting from one day to one week. During a stay, you will learn the story of Korean Buddhism, temple etiquette and Zen meditation, *cham-seon*, while also partaking of a tea ceremony, *dado*, and (attempting!) the 108 bows.

I discovered Templestay in South Korea quite by accident. On my first night in Seoul, jet-lagged and unable to sleep, I found myself watching television at 3am. I was mesmerised by an "infomercial" for Templestay, featuring a Western couple wandering around ancient temples in the Korean mountains.

"Do you feel drained and burned out? Are you overworked and constantly tired? Enjoy a rejuvenating visit to a Templestay" said the advertisement voiceover.

I was excited by the idea of disconnecting from my busy life. I needed a window of time to reflect and reboot, and crucially, to turn off my devices.

I immediately picked up the phone and dialled the concierge.

"Can you arrange a Templestay visit for me? I have to go!"

"Of course. Our pleasure."

I was booked in to go by the following morning.

Templestay Center
Address: 56, Ujeongguk-ro, Jongno-gu, Seoul
Website: www.eng.templestay.com

Shift your energy

It was mid-January and I was the only guest. I was at the 1700-year-old Jeondeungsa Temple in Incheon, one of the oldest in Korea. Legend says it was built by the three sons of the founder of the first Korean kingdom of Gojoseon as a shrine to their ancestors.

Located on the top of Mount Jeongjoksan, the temple is made up of ten wooden buildings of different architectural styles ranging from the first dynasty to the mid-Joseon dynasty. Delicate carvings and 800-year-old paintings of Korean landscapes and the Buddha decorate each building. The temple might feel like a museum, but it is home to a thriving, working Buddhist community.

Most Temples provide clothing for visitors, and I happily put on the large quilted pink vest and purple balloon pants. Even though I thought I looked like a circus clown, I was the most comfortable I'd been in years!

Make sure to bring extra clothes, toiletries and hiking boots, especially if you visit in the autumn or winter. Wear wool and layers of clothes as the weather goes from extremely cold at night to sunny and warm in the afternoon, depending on the location.

You can do as much or as little as you like. Even though there is electricity and an internet connection, it's a good idea to leave electronic-communication devices turned off. They aren't forbidden but the point of getting away, after all, is getting away.

Communal showers and bathrooms are clean and adequate; but don't expect a "luxury spa" experience. Bring your own soap and towels.

It is required that you take off your shoes before entering each building, so bring sturdy slippers or loafers – easy to take off and put on.

Bedtime is early but there is electricity in all the rooms, so you can read. Be prepared to share a room with a stranger if the Templestay is crowded.

Cameras are allowed and you can photograph almost everywhere in the grounds.

Children are welcome, and there are special programmes for families, which you can find out about from each temple.

Everything at the temple felt so nurturing, from the mountain air to the spring water that flows from stone fountains and tastes better than any fine wine. This, combined with some vigorous hiking and quiet meditation, ensured that I experienced deep restful sleep every night.

Feed your soul

The best way to learn about Korean monastic culture is to experience the food. Temple food is vegetarian, nutritious and prepared with care to "cleanse" the body and soul. Meals are taken in silence and you are encouraged to eat mindfully and moderately. According to Buddhist teaching, eating is part of the journey to enlightenment and must be done respectfully – which means finishing everything on your plate, so as not to leave any waste and to show gratitude to those who cooked for you.

Their tenet of using locally sourced, seasonal, plant-based food feels remarkably on trend. You may have thought society's current focus on plant-based diets, slow food and eating seasonally was a modern invention, but Korea's Buddhists have been practising this for centuries – 1600 years to be precise. Their approach to food can be summed up in the formal monastic meal, *barugongyang*: wooden bowls containing tofu, porridge, rice, greens, vegetables, soups and kimchi are placed on the table and everyone helps themselves to just the right amount.

The idea is to feed your body in readiness for spiritual practice, as well as work. Korean monks and nuns don't eat garlic, leeks, chives or onions, as they are too astringent and thought to interfere with focus during meditation.

If you are in Korea but unable to make it to a temple for a visit, you can still experience traditional temple food at the Seoul restaurant Balwoo Gongyang, whose chefs have trained under monks. Or you can learn to prepare the dishes yourself. The Korean Temple Food Center, also in Seoul, runs cooking classes.

Jeondeungsa Temple
Address: 37-41, Jeondeungsa-ro, Gilsang-myeon, Ganghwa-gun
Website: www.jeondeungsa.org

Korean Temple Food Center
Address: 56 Ujeongkuk-ro Jongno-gu Seoul
Website: www.koreatemplefood.com

Balwoo Gongyang Restaurant
Address: Fifth Floor, 56 Ujeongguk-ro, Jongno-gu Seoul
Website: www.eng.balwoo.or.kr

108 bows

I was determined to join the 4am prayer service. I sat in the small, quiet temple and observed two monks bowing and chanting, and three lay workers performing the 108 deep-bow ceremony after the service. These bows are strenuous physical work. You must touch five points of your body – knees, elbows, forehead – to the floor. They are designed to purify your mind and atone for the excesses of your ego, such as selfishness, anger or envy.

I watched an older woman bowing like an acrobat. My own attempts were less than successful.

Later on, I got talking to a man about the 108 bows and how hard I had found it to perform even one correctly.

"It is very difficult to do the deep bows; one must practise for many years," he assured me, adding that the goal was intention, not perfection.

And that was my lesson. Spiritual practice is not a competition. Every attempt you make is meaningful. The objective is to keep going and with that, growing.

The deep bow mantra

The deep bow is usually done at the beginning and end of a service. Start with a standing bow, and then continue into a kneeling position. Separate your hands and place them palms up, either side of your forehead. Continue bowing, until your hands and forehead touch the floor. Then raise your hands above your ears before returning them to the floor. This bow is an act of humility in front of the Buddha. Typically, as you bow you demand of yourself, among other things, the following:

To be humble
To be thankful at all times
To eliminate selfishness
To appreciate parents and family
To appreciate body and soul

> To give thanks for being alive
>
> To respect your teachers
>
> To be more forgiving
>
> To be slow to anger
>
> To be kind to all

We are happy now

I was invited to take tea with a monk, along with a translator. I confided how stressful my life had been in the previous year, as my husband had undergone (and fully recuperated from) complex surgery. I started to cry. The monk didn't miss a beat. Before hearing my translated words, he changed the topic.

"We are happy now," he said soothingly.

Translation: I was wasting precious moments of the present carrying the stress of the past. Perspective was all.

"Yes, of course! We are happy now," I repeated, and suddenly asked myself, why was I crying? I had travelled thousands of miles to get myself up to this mountain temple and sit before this monk in one of the most beautiful places on earth. The message was profound yet so simple.

To this day, I rely on that moment to get through a situation when I am stressed, worried or scared. I recall the monk's words and I say to myself, "We are happy now", because it's true. We can always choose to focus on gratitude and joy, no matter the circumstances.

Make a friend

Before I left Seoul for the temple, a colleague gave me this advice: "Make a friend." The suggestion underscores how much bonding and community – *jeong* – are strong tenets of Korean culture.

I was a little baffled at how to do this, to be honest. I was supposed to eat and meditate in silence at the temple. Yet after arriving, I went for a walk, armed with my camera. It was a beautiful, crisp morning. Suddenly, I heard a man ask, "Would you like me to take your picture?"

He introduced himself, telling me he was at the temple just for the day to recharge. We ended up hiking and taking tea, talking about life in New York and Korea. I did indeed make a friend. Not only did I learn how Koreans use Buddhist temples as retreats (even for a day) from their hectic lives, but how much richer your visit to a country is when spending time with someone local.

Unmunsa, the Cloud Gate Temple

One of the most awe-inspiring Buddhist temples is Unmunsa (the Cloud Gate Temple), which is nestled in the south of the Taebaek Mountains. Built around 560 AD, it was partly destroyed during a Japanese invasion in the sixteenth century. The temple complex was rebuilt during the eighteenth century, and today the site contains a traditional pavilion (used for gatherings) and shrine halls. Unmunsa is also the largest training college for Buddhist nuns (*bhikkhunis*) in Korea, with about 300 live-in students enrolled on the four-year course. Women come from all over the world to dedicate their lives to the study of Buddhism. When I visited, I met a young nun in training from Brooklyn!

Unmunsa's beauty is magnificent. Surrounded by stunning forest, rivers and hills, the temple is also home to a number of national treasures that have been officially recognised (for having exceptional artistic, cultural and historical value to the country), including a 400-year-old weeping pine tree, a three-storey stone pagoda, and a seated stone Buddha. Also look out for the two-centuries-old ginkgo trees whose fruit the nuns collect and pickle.

Kyung-sook Shin had been invited to Unmunsa to speak to a class of students. I went along to accompany her. We left very early, travelling many hours by train and then car from Seoul to the temple. When we arrived, we were greeted by the director of the college and head nun. I was bleary-eyed, and needed a caffeine fix immediately.

Normally, when I get up in the morning, I am not awake until I have had two cups of coffee. I groan and wander like a ghost from bed to kitchen until that first sip of caffeine slides down my throat.

I asked the director if I could get a cup of coffee. She said yes, and a short while later brought me a life-saving cup. At the time I didn't know it was inappropriate to ask for coffee – nuns don't drink coffee, only herbal teas. It was like I'd requested the vegan nuns prepare a burger for lunch. They believe consumption of caffeine will disturb the tranquillity and meditative atmosphere of the temple.

Now I see how unbelievably kind this small gesture was. She understood I was a New Yorker who craved her coffee fix, and graciously served me.

Many temples also do not have Western toilets. I have had my share of using outhouses in Asia so when I was in need, I asked the director if there was a bathroom I might use. She most kindly allowed me to use her personal (Western) toilet and I was never so happy in my life.

The class of 50 students were utterly delighted by Kyung-sook. She talked about her work as a writer, and everyone was spellbound. We also had the privilege of meeting several nuns, some of whom gave us a tour of their favourite sites in the temple grounds. For one, it was a flowering cherry tree where she went to think and pray; for another, it was the vegetable garden which she tended and loved.

And one nun not only showed us the famous pine tree; she hugged it, thankful for all it provides. I hugged it too – it was like embracing a grandmother. I swear I felt it hug me back!

My favourite place in the temple grounds was the cold stream that flowed through it. Trees and flowers graced both banks, and if you followed it along the hill and crossed a bridge, you came across a small pagoda where you could sit and meditate.

Walking barefoot in the cool water and jumping over the rocks from one side to the other, I couldn't stop laughing and realised I was experiencing a natural high. I felt giddy and ecstatic, fully in the moment. My mind was just there, calm, without an ounce of worry. This feeling stayed with me for the rest of the day.

At the end of our tour, we were shown Unmunsa's little museum, which is filled with embroidered objects, paintings, paper handcrafts and other artworks the women have created, revealing the amazing female energy and sense of community within the temple.

Mindful living

Even in a short visit you can see and learn a lot. The joy of the nuns was palpable, their devotion to a life of loving kindness and meditation an example for all of us. You can see how their happiness, their *heung*, comes from simply doing and being – they don't need piles of "stuff" to enrich their lives.

A key element of Korean Buddhism is Zen meditation, the practice of quieting the mind through breath work. Seated in either the lotus or cross-legged position, you have to focus on breathing rhythmically while paying attention to all the feelings and thoughts that arise. When your mind "chatters" (and it will), you are instructed to redirect it by letting thoughts go and returning to your breathing.

In recent years, modern scientific research has proven what Buddhist monks and nuns have long known: meditation reduces stress, increases focus and creativity and boosts your memory. It also builds acceptance of yourself and others, quieting that critical, worrying mind.

When we drove away, I was filled with gratitude for the lessons Unmunsa had given me.

I may not be able to shave my head, wear robes and study Buddhism day and night – but I can hug a tree anywhere to feel the power of nature and my place in the scheme of all things.

Seeing the nuns carry out each day with mindfulness was a lesson in expressing gratitude for all the gifts in my own life. The peaceful and loving atmosphere of the place highlighted the importance of taking a break, and the healing power of immersion in beauty and tranquillity.

Even if you can only manage a day trip to Unmunsa, you will be surprised by how much stepping away from your routine and immersing yourself in this beautiful place will nurture you.

Unmunsa Temple
Address: 264, Unmunsa-gil, Unmun-myeon, Cheongdo-gun, Gyeongsangbuk-do
Website: www.unmunsa.or.kr

Lessons in happiness from a Buddhist temple

• Taking time out is important, but you don't need to go away to do it. Turn your home into a temple. Cook nourishing food, wear loose clothes, open your windows and turn off the screen. Take a walk in nature and meditate.

• Appreciate the moment; don't get dragged down by the past. We are happy now.

• Silence and meditation are medicine for the mind.

• Go at your own pace. Don't compare yourself to others. It's not a competition.

• Drink tea to warm the body and quiet your chattering brain.

• Eat plant-based, non-processed food. Try to eat vegetarian, even if it's only once a week.

• Treat food as fuel for your body; don't overindulge or be wasteful.

• Make a friend. Connection is important. All friendships enrich you.

Soybean
Paste Stew

된장찌개

(Doenjang-jjigae)

For my friend Kyung-sook Shin, soybean paste – *doenjang* – is more than a simple ingredient, it's a stand-alone health food.

"Soybean paste is made from *maeju*, a block of fermented soybeans, which resembles the Japanese miso but tastes distinctly different. Nowadays, most Koreans are open to store-bought soybean paste, but back in the day, Korean families had an annual rite of making their own.

"This staple Korean paste, not surprisingly, is also mentioned in my book, *Please Look After Mom*, and it happened that a European edition mistranslated *doenjang* as miso, and I remember explaining the difference between the two.

"We Koreans treat this soybean paste as a bit of a pan-

110

acea. We eat clear soybean paste soup when our stomach feels mildly upset, and even slather scars with the paste to help them heal faster. It has a very particular odour due to its fermenting process, which might put off someone who hasn't grown up with it as most Koreans do.

"The conventional soybean paste is made purely from soybeans and nothing else, and the most common ingredients for the stew include courgettes, radishes, mushrooms, and a generous amount of diced tofu, so it's second to none when it comes to protein content. I wouldn't be the only Korean to say that this soybean paste is the secret to Korean wellbeing."

Ingredients
(Serves 2–3)

Handful dried ancho-
vies or 1 tbsp anchovy
powder
3 strips kombu kelp
(each piece the size of a
credit card)
Pinch crushed dried red
pepper (optional)
½ courgette, seeds
scooped out
200g tofu
2–3 shiitake mushrooms
(or one pine mushroom)
½ potato
½ onion
4-5 cheongyang red
peppers
1 red chilli pepper
1 tbsp garlic paste
1 tbsp sesame oil
2 tbsp soybean paste
½ tbsp red pepper paste
1 large spring onion,
white part only, finely
chopped, to garnish
1 tbsp honey

1. First you need to make your stock: fill a saucepan with 1.5 litres of water and bring it to the boil, then reduce the heat and add the dried anchovies, kombu kelp and a pinch of dried red pepper flakes, if you like a bit of spice.

2. Simmer the stock over a medium heat until it has turned the colour of pale beer. This will usually take 5–10 minutes. Don't leave it any longer or the kelp will turn gelatinous and make the stock a bit slimy. An alternative method is to soak all the ingredients sit in lukewarm water for an hour.

3. While the stock is simmering (or stewing), chop the courgette, tofu, mushrooms, and potato into small cubes. Finely dice the onion, chilli pepper and cheongyang red peppers.

4. Put the garlic paste in a saucepan and stir-fry it with the sesame oil over a low heat.

5. Add the diced onions to the garlic paste and keep stirring.

6. Turn up the heat and add, in this order, the potato, courgette, mushrooms, cheongyang red peppers and tofu to the pan.

7. Stir the soybean paste, diced chilli pepper and red pepper paste into the vegetables and continue to stir-fry until they have softened.

8. Pour in 200ml of the pre-prepared anchovy stock and bring it to the boil.

9. When the stock gets dense and sticky add the chopped spring onions.

10. Spoon the stew into a Korean hotpot bowl if you have one; if you don't, a regular bowl will do. Drizzle over the honey and serve it with a plate of steamed cabbage.

Destination:
Busan

Wellness

안녕

Annyeong

The Barcelona of Korea

If you take the train from Seoul to the coastal city of Busan, you'll be there in about two and a half hours, and I promise you won't be attacked by zombie vampires like in the hit movie, *Train to Busan*. Although it did put Korea's second-largest city on the map, Busan is the opposite of a horror film. A port town with gorgeous beaches, hip restaurants and the cultural cachet of the Busan International Film Festival, it's been dubbed the Barcelona of Korea. It's also the wellness capital of the country.

For art lovers, Busan is an absolute revelation. Unlike many other cities in the world, graffiti artists are celebrated in Busan. As part of a government initiative called "Dreaming of Busan Machu Picchu", artists were actively encouraged to cover the streets with their creativity, transforming a once dilapidated slum into a colourful and vibrant neighbourhood. Known as the Gamcheon Culture Village, its small houses, built in tiers up the steep hills overlooking Busan, are now a mish-mash of pastel colours, and the tiny alleyways are full of painted murals. This love and appreciation of art has naturally brought global artists to exhibit here, including Amsterdam-based Adele Renault, famous for painting massive murals of pigeons, Spanish painter Eva Armisen and British contemporary artist Julian Opie.

Busan Gamcheon Culture Village
Address: 203, Gamnae 2-ro Saha-gu, Busan
www.gamcheon.or.kr

The art of healing

If the 21st century has a buzzword, it must be "wellness". Taking care of yourself through herbal medicine, nutrition and massage is no longer prac-tised only by those we once labelled "health nuts". Today, wellness is every-where, a high-powered CEO is just as likely to sing the praises of sauna and meditation as your yoga teacher. For Koreans, watching this wellness craze unfold must be curious indeed.

Despite being a culture that moves at warp speed, it's also one with deep roots in the practice of healing and wellness. In fact, everything the world is now embracing has been a core part of Korean life for 5000 years.

In Busan, the practice of wellness could qualify as an art form, almost as much as the murals on the walls. The city is devoted to it, boasting the highest density of *jimjilbang*, bathhouse spas, in Korea – around 450. A staple of Korean life, the *jimjilbang* is a 24-hour, gender-separated bathhouse with a vast array of pamper-ing facilities, including soaking pools, saunas and massage tables.

The largest and most luxurious one in Busan is Spa Land, located inside

Shinsegae Department Store Centum City, also the largest shopping centre in the world. The thermal water in Spa Land's baths and pools is pumped in from two hot springs that lie 1000 metres underground. One spring contains calcium chloride, the other sodium chloride, both said to help with skin, circulation and relieving nerve and back pain. There are eighteen different hot spring baths at different temperatures, and thirteen themed saunas, a salt room, an ice room and a pyramid room to absorb cosmic energy. Even Koreans are said to be awestruck by it.

Spa Land Centum City
Address: 35 Centumnam-daero, Haeundae-gu, Busan
Website: www.shinsegae.com

Soak, sauna, massage

Asking people in the West to make time to relax is not as easy as it sounds. We know taking time out is essential to prevent burnout, but many worry that if they do so it will be seen as laziness. In Korea, it's the opposite. The art of relaxation is displayed to its full potential at the *jimjilbang*, where Koreans might spend all day to rest, recuperate and restore their energy levels.

Studies are clear that relaxation boosts your immune system, reduces stress and tension and improves your productivity and concentration. Taking saunas can lower blood pressure, ease headaches and boost endorphins.

There is a Korean belief that you are not truly friends with someone until you visit a bathhouse together! You are required to be naked, but don't worry – everyone else is too and nobody stares. Once there, you will find baths of different water temperatures to help with circulation and muscles, and some may also be filled with herbs or salts. The saunas also use Himalayan salt to improve circulation, or jade to help with arthritis. Massages are given in steam rooms to clear the body of toxins.

My first visit to a Korean spa was for a massage, and it was something I will never forget. I walked into a warm steam room completely made of stone. The masseuse was a small woman wearing a two-piece bathing suit and she was all business, washing me down and dry-brushing my body with what felt like a lawn rake. Then came a bristle brush before she began to massage me with warm oil and the most intense hands, penetrating deeply into my muscles and tissue. Later that night I slept so well, when I woke I was filled with energy and joy.

....

Another memorable restorative spa moment and perhaps one of my most unique adventures into wellness happened after I spent the day with friends climbing 1000 steps up to the Bomunsa Temple, located on the Sangbong-san Mountain on Seokomodo Island. At the end of the trail, a *maaeseok-buljwasang*, a seated Buddha statue carved into rock, was waiting for us. We made wishes in front of the 33-foot-high figure and then headed back down. My feet were so sore and hot by the end I could barely take another step. My friends steered me towards an outdoor communal foot spa nearby in the countryside.

Man-made but built around natural hot springs, these free, outdoor foot spas can be found all over Korea. Sit on either a wooden bench or stone ledge while you dangle your feet in the waters rich with magnesium, calcium and sodium – said to aid with pain and arthritis.

I plunged my feet and legs into the flowing water as it bubbled up and instantly I was restored.

Ten steps to glowing skin

Along with K-pop and K-drama, the other Korean phenomenon that has taken off like a rocket is K-beauty. And for good reason. Koreans have beautiful, luminous skin – they idealise a skin type known as *chok-chok*: plump, dewy and youthful. In the West, we've focused on enhancing our faces with make-up, but the Korean way is all about creating a beautiful canvas to begin with. The secret? Incredible beauty products and a 10-step skincare regime designed to keep the skin hydrated.

Have you used cleansers, face masks or moisturisers by Amorepacific, Cosrx, Innisfee or Sulwhasoo? All Korean. K-beauty products are praised for their high-tech research and development, pure ingredients and effectiveness.

The Korean 10-step skincare regime starts young. Korean children are taught to cleanse, moisturise and use SPF. By the time they are eighteen, a skincare routine that takes 30 minutes each day is integral to their lives. Sheet masks, serums, essence and BB creams aren't a luxury, but a must on Korean shelves. This multi-layered approach to skincare was first developed in the 1960s. But times are changing, and beauty brands are producing multi-tasking products that are just as effective as two separate steps.

Try the Korean 10-step skincare routine

Step 1: Oil Cleanser
Massage oil cleanser in a circular motion into dry skin to remove make-up. Rinse off with warm water.

Step 2: Foam or Gel Cleanser
Use one pump of foam or gel cleanser and massage in a circular motion into your damp face, rinse off with warm water.

Step 3: Exfoliator

Dot facial scrub or peeling gel on your face, massage in a circular motion, rinse off. (1–3 times per week).

Step 4: Toner

Toner is used to remove particles of cleanser or scrub that may remain on the skin. Using a cotton pad, wipe it across your face.

Step 5: Essence

Essences are liquids with active ingredients to increase hydration. Dot on your face and pat into your skin.

Step 6: Serum Treatments

Korean serums are concentrated liquids infused with vitamins or acids to repair the skin. Dot on your face and smooth into your skin.

Step 7: Sheet Masks

Place ingredient-soaked paper or fabric face mask over your face and leave on for 15 minutes.

Step 8: Eye Cream

Dot eye cream beneath your eyes.

Step 9: Moisturiser

Dot and massage into your face to keep your skin hydrated.

Step 10: Sunscreen

Dot on your face and pat into your skin.

I think another reason Korean women have such excellent skin is their diet, which consists mostly of vegetables, fruits, roots and soups; they only eat meat and other protein in small amounts.

When I first visited Korea, I went to the Sulwhasoo Flagship Store in Gangnam, the largest skincare shop in the country, for a facial. All its products contain the healing herb Korean ginseng – for its anti-ageing properties. The shop has a display of original creams and lotions produced by founder Suh Sung-whan's mother in the 1930s. All I can say is, after my facial, I walked out looking like I was 25 and feeling like I was walking on air!

Koreans are daring when it comes to skincare and will use ingredients you wouldn't believe would end up on your bathroom shelf, let alone your face. Donkey milk moisture cream for your face? Yes! Seahorses? Absolutely! Studies show seahorses contain antioxidant and anti-inflammatory properties. Jeju Island (see Chapter 8) is home to the largest seahorse farm in the world. I was honoured to take a tour with its founder, Noh Sum, who began studying seahorses for their medicinal qualities before applying his research to the skincare line, Rarita, which is manufactured on the island. He told me that the seahorse extract cream and masks were initially developed for his wife, who has highly sensitive skin. When I met his wife, her complexion was flawless. She looked 30, although she was in fact 50.

The seahorses are farmed in a building filled with hundreds of tanks of Jeju ocean water. They are then dried, refined and mixed with marine collagen among other ingredients, to make antioxidant creams and masks. Naturally, I couldn't wait to try out the products. It was like putting velvet on my face; a thin, moist cream of Jeju Island sea velvet. My skin and complexion never felt smoother.

But if you think seahorses aren't enough in your quest for perfect skin, how about a Korean gold facial, which uses real 24-carat gold-foil masks and serums? Practitioners claim gold removes toxins and tightens the skin (although no clinical research confirms this).

And it would be remiss of me not to mention the Korean vaginal "facial", a herbal steam of your private parts with the promise of relieving menstrual cramps. This one, which may be offered at the *jimjilbang* bathhouse, is truly for the bravest of the brave.

Sulwhasoo Flagship Store
Address: 18 Dosan-daero 45-gil, Sinsa-dong, Gangnam-gu, Seoul
Website: www.sulwhasoo.com

Barbie mania and *Vampire's Kiss*

When I was a little girl, I loved playing with my Barbie doll, as did millions of kids around the world. I play-acted being a teacher with my Barbie, wanting to emulate my mother, who was one. I loved changing her outfits, and my friends and I created little scenes and stories with our dolls, feeding our imaginations. They were our avatars at the age of six; and then we grew up.

As an adult, I first became a filmmaker, and produced the cult classic *Vampire's Kiss* with Nicolas Cage, now considered one of the actor's most formidable roles. Never in my wildest dreams could I imagine that one day millions of women, young and old, especially in Korea, would try to make themselves look like my childhood doll through surgery. Or that the Korean vampire facial, which injects your own blood (after extracting the plasma) into your face to stimulate collagen, would start a global beauty revolution!

Korea has the highest rate of plastic surgery procedures per capita in the world. A Gallup survey found that one in every three women in Korea between the ages of 19 and 29 have had plastic surgery. It's ironic that the country is also steeped in Zen Buddhism, which advocates acceptance. Korea has the longest life expectancy for women in the world, and one of its mantras is "imperfection is perfection". Despite this, the subways of Seoul are plastered with advertisements for plastic surgery showing before and after pictures and promoting a Barbie-perfect face that will never age. This pressure to look forever young in Korea is intense, and I believe harmful.

Korea's plastic surgery craze started after the Korean War, when UN and US military doctors performed reconstructive surgery on victims of the war. Since then, the practice has surged, boosted today by a competitive job market and the K-pop and K-drama phenomenon, *hallyu*. The stars have surgery and their fans follow. The most popular surgeries in Korea today are double eye lifts, cheek and chin bone sculpting, breast implants and nose jobs.

Foreigners are now coming to Korea for surgery because of its innovative, minimally invasive techniques. There are so many plastic surgery tourists that Seoul's Incheon International Airport once considered opening a cosmetic surgery centre inside the terminal. (Doctors rejected the idea, fearing patients, who needed to be monitored after surgery, would try to board flights immediately. Flying could also cause stitches to come loose due to a difference in air pressure.)

Now, growing up, I adored my grandmother Becky, whom I considered a natural beauty. She always exercised, ate healthily, and only used soap and water on her face. She did dye her hair blonde when she turned grey, but that was the extent of her beauty regime. Until she died at a ripe old age, Becky was beautiful.

A few years ago, my younger sister was regularly getting Botox shots, and begged me to do the same. She said the lines between my eyes were appalling! I insisted that I'd earned the lines on my face. I reminded her of Becky. But my sister was persistent, and I relented. I had a Botox shot and frankly, I didn't see any difference.

The next morning, however, was a different story. I woke up to find a huge lake of fluid had formed under my eye. What had I done? I called my sister, who reassured me my face would return to normal, which it did, after two weeks. That has been my one experience with a non-surgical procedure, and I have vowed, never again.

Of course, as I age I notice new lines and wrinkles, and fret about my chin. Is it double now? Where did all those brown spots come from on my arms and legs? Am I turning into a Dalmatian? I see the changes to my body and face, but I choose to practise the Korean Buddhist way of acceptance and contentment. Instead of a vampire facial, I prefer to take a cold plunge in an outdoor swimming pond or the ocean, which also tightens my skin, keeps it glowing and energises my entire being.

There is no quick or lasting way to look like I did when I was twenty. Instead, I embrace every year of my life, and remind myself of the wise monk's words, "We are happy now".

I feel sad when I read about how many Korean teens and young women want to become human Barbie dolls. Our natural faces and bodies distinguish us and make us individuals. The plastic surgery frenzy is creating a population of sameness where soon we will only be able to differentiate ourselves with a fingerprint. I hope the craze abates and the Korean pursuit of beauty pivots to focus on health, drawing on the traditional Korean practice of bringing the body into balance.

Tea elixir

I believe another secret behind Korean's great skin and good health is tea.

I learned to drink tea on my numerous trips to England, but drinking tea in Korea is a whole different experience. This is not your cup of PG Tips.

Can you imagine sipping a cup of seahorse tea? Well, I did. It was surprisingly refreshing and sophisticated in its taste, with a slight herbal, even sweet accent. I would highly recommend it!

Many teas in Korea are made from trees, roots and herbs found only locally, and are prized for their medicinal properties. People drink it both at the beginning and end of the day. It is also taken before meditation, and as a healing drink while resting. Plum tea is one of the most popular teas and is drunk after meals. Koreans believe plum tea helps with fatigue and as a detoxifier. Jujube fruit tea is also popular, considered helpful in guarding against colds and reducing fever.

My favourite is pine needle tea, *sollip-cha,* which I first sipped in one of the oldest tea houses in Seoul. (It is served mostly at traditional tea houses rather than street cafés.) It had a clean, crisp, citrus taste, with the familiar scent of pine trees. Made from either fresh, dried or fermented needles of the Korean red pine, it contains four times as much vitamin C as a glass of fresh orange juice and is also high in vitamin A. It works as a decongestant and is good for sore throats, but is not recommended for pregnant women. I have also drunk iced pine needle tea on ferociously hot summer days while hiking and it was incredibly refreshing. Kyung-sook Shin, says the moment she takes a sip of pine needle tea, she feels as if she were at a temple in the deep forest.

Herbs and diet

Life expectancy in Korea is set to hit 90 for women and 84 for men – the highest of any country in the world. One of the reasons for this can be found inside Korean kitchens: in the aforementioned fermented pickles and cabbage dish, kimchi. Full of vitamins and probiotics for good digestion, it was recently labelled one of the world's healthiest foods by Health.com.

Okay, there might be another secret weapon too. (Why stop at one?) The root herb Korean ginseng included in the delicious soup recipe in Chapter 1. Eaten raw, taken as powder or in tea, it's the Swiss Army knife of herbs, said to boost your liver and immune system, fight fatigue, reduce inflammation and for men, improve erectile dysfunction.

While Western medicine is practised widely, Koreans also frequently turn to *hanyak*, traditional Korean medicine, for small ailments. *Hanuihak* takes a holistic approach to the human body, using a combination of herbal remedies (in the form of teas, powders and ointments) and acupuncture. Although influenced initially by traditional Chinese medicine, over the centuries *hanuihak* has developed its own methods and practices.

My colleague Sue Park remembers going to see a *hanyak* herbalist or acupuncturist pretty often when growing up in Korea. "I think Korean people go to the doctor when they feel they have a serious health condition, or have been in accidents or have actual injuries," she notes.

"It is usually when you have milder problems that you go to the herbalist, or when you want to keep in shape or maintain a healthier lifestyle and diet."

Sue says there is an infinite list of what you could be prescribed by an herbalist: "Stag's horn to bear gall bladder, ginseng, ginger, all kinds of plants and weird stuff... I think it really depends on the herbal concoction. Each one is customised for every patient, so ingredients are different for each person and each occasion."

One place to add to your wellness itinerary in Korea is Donguibogam Village in Sancheong, a theme park where the "theme" is herbal medicine. Here you can tune your energy in the Hanbang "Chi" (life force) Experience Center, learn the 5000-year-old history of Korean healing in the Museum of Herbal Medicine, then eat a meal cooked with medicinal herbs.

Sancheong Donguibogam Village
Address: 45-6 #555 Road, Donguibogam-ro, Sancheong-gun, Gyeongnam
Website: www.donguibogam-village.sancheong.go.kr

Body and breath

My antennae are always up, especially when I travel. What I am going to uncover next?

One afternoon, I was strolling around Mullae-dong, a neighbourhood that used to be the industrial area of Seoul. Today it's become hip and cool, filled with art galleries, boutiques and restaurants. Suddenly, one small white building caught my attention.

I looked in through the window and saw a row of white ceramic sculptures of the human body in different poses. Mmmm? A doctor's office? Then I spied posters depicting bodies in different postures. I thought it must be a really cool yoga studio. I practise yoga, so headed straight in.

I discovered it was not yoga, but a Kouk Sun Do studio. Also known as Sundo, it's a Taoist holistic meditation practice that uses "deep abdominal energy centre breathing" with movements that develop body, mind and spirit. It sounded very much like yoga to me, so I was interested. As luck would have it, a class was about to start and I was welcome to join. As I didn't have the correct clothes (a jacket and pants similar to a martial arts uniform), they offered to loan me an outfit.

Before the class started, I perused the studio bookshelves. A thought flashed through my mind that I might be the first Western person to ever discover this nearly 10,000-year-old practice. Being me, I bought every book I could, filled my arms with posters and tried to buy one of the little sculptures which unfortunately weren't for sale. I couldn't wait to tell my friends about this. Yoga was already a billion-dollar industry. Sundo could be the next best thing!

Before the class I squeezed myself into an outfit so small it barely covered my behind. As I entered the room, I was petrified the pant seams might burst any second. I joined ten students, already advanced practitioners of Sundo. The class was in Korean so I had to figure it out by watching others. As my classmates rolled around like rollypoly dolls, it became clear Sundo is not yoga. The movements felt very off-kilter to me, and I found myself simply rolling around rather than into a posture that you were supposed to hold while breathing.

Somehow I made it through the hour-class. I was sweating, but at least my outfit was intact and frankly, that was my biggest concern. While I may not have mastered the movements, I was thrilled to have discovered this ancient meditative art form.

I left the studio and raced to my friend Kyung-sook Shin's home, where we were having dinner. Like me, Kyung-sook has been practising yoga for years (and is soon to publish a book about her yoga practice). I proudly showed her all the material I'd purchased, then described the class and my attempt to master even one pose.

"Honestly, I thought the seams in my outfit would burst," I confessed.

She started laughing and couldn't stop.

"Barbara, true, it's an old practice but no one does it!" she said, while making me a soothing cup of tea.

We had a beautiful meal and were in hysterics throughout about my latest adventure in Korea.

The healing forest

As we know, hiking is a national pastime in Korea (see Chapter 5), where being active is prized. Knowing the therapeutic value of being in nature, Koreans have taken it to the next level, planting ecological healing forests throughout the country to encourage *salim yok*, "forest bathing".

The Busan Healing Forest, on the outskirts of Ahopsan Mountain, opened in 2017 and its purpose is right there in the name – to provide space for healing. The forest contains many trails you can follow, or you can join activities like tea drinking, meditation and guided walks to learn about healing plants.

All that is required in forest bathing is to walk slowly though the forest to activate your five senses, breathe deeply and enjoy the scenery. It's as easy as it sounds and better yet, the benefits are incredible. Research has shown time in a forest reduces stress, boosts your immune system and generates feelings of wellbeing and positivity. It's a gift to yourself wrapped up in the scent of pine.

Lessons in wellness

- What you put in your body determines your health. If you want to be strong and live long, you must eat healthfully.
- Skincare should be part of your daily routine.
- Tea is medicinal, calming the mind and detoxifying the body.
- Go forest bathing. It will boost your immunity and make you happy inside and out.
- A massage or sauna should not be a luxury but a weekly activity. It will lower blood pressure, increase endorphins and lower stress and anxiety.
- Wellness is not a fad, but a lifelong practice.
- Outdoor exercise, whichever kind you enjoy, is an essential ingredient for your health and longevity.

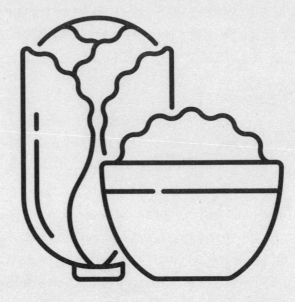

This recipe was given to me by Dongkyung Lee, the mother of my associate Sue Park. Interestingly, she wasn't a fan of kimchi at first.

"I grew up eating my mother's Gyeongsang-style cabbage kimchi, known to be extremely salty since it makes use of various salted seafoods. I'm from Ulsan, a port city within the Gyeongsang province, where the local speciality is *jeotgal* – different sorts of seafood including squid, oysters, anchovies and fish eggs, fermented with ample amounts of salt. This star side dish is so moreish that it is called 'thieves of steamed rice', since you will wolf down bowl after bowl of steamed rice, without even realising it, when it's topped with *jeotgal*.

"Each province, not to mention each different family,

boasts a drastically different recipe for cabbage kimchi, and the conventional Gyeongsang-style kimchi always contains *jeotgal* which makes it the saltiest kimchi in the country.

"As much as I love seafood and cabbage kimchi with seafood twists, they have a very specific aftertaste, and it's not for everyone. I never confessed this to my own mother, but I never loved that aftertaste.

"So when I first got married, I refused to make kimchi myself; it's a long and arduous process, and if I'm not able to fully enjoy it, why go to all that effort? But when I visited my older sister and tasted her homemade cabbage kimchi – so different from our mother's – it completely blew my mind. She married a man from a different southern province known for its cuisine and she adopted some of his hometown's ingredients and variations in order to rid her cabbage kimchi of that strong Gyeongsang aftertaste. Her kimchi had this unique, healthy tang to it that really cleansed my palate, and I just couldn't stop helping myself to it!

"She taught me her recipe, and I've revised it over the years in order to tailor it to my family's tastes. This recipe was born of multiple different Korean local cultures, my personal preferences and years of tweaks.

"The kimchi-making and fermenting process is notoriously complicated and usually not one person's job – it used to be a communal, intergenerational event. I have tried to simplify the steps but I know the recipe still looks intimidating, although, believe me when I say, it's boiled down to the essentials!"

Ingredients

(Makes 15kg of kimchi;
to make smaller amounts
divide the ingredients by
the number of cabbages
you wish to ferment.)

5 medium-sized radishes
10 medium-sized
Chinese cabbages,
unwashed

Sticky rice sauce

3 dried apples, sliced
10 dried shiitake
mushrooms
10 dried dates, pitted
100g dried radishes
100g dried kombu
500g sweet rice powder

Shrimp paste marinade

10 garlic bulbs, peeled
5 onions, peeled and
quartered
50g root ginger, peeled
2 Korean pears, core
removed
300g salted, pickled
shrimps
20 raw frozen shrimps,
peeled
500ml fish sauce
1.5kg dried red
pepper flakes

Seasonings

20 spring onions
20 chives
Sea salt; this is the only
salt used for kimchi

Equipment

2 big bowls for the
salting process
Food processor
3–4 big (5kg), clean
plastic containers for the
fermenting process
(sterilise them by
washing them in your
dishwasher or just
wash thoroughly and
rack-dry)

Day 1

(Start in the late afternoon/early evening)

1. Firstly, wash the radishes thoroughly and cut
each of them into 8 pieces. Then put them in
a big bowl with about 200g salt. Let them sit
overnight (for 12 hours), stirring every 3 hours
or so to ensure the salt is spread evenly.

2. For the cabbages, it is crucial you don't wash them until after the salting process. Cut each cabbage in half vertically and leave them in a big bowl full of salted water, also for 12 hours. The water should be seawater-salty. After the first 6 hours, you should turn over the cabbages so they soak up the salted water evenly.

3. Meanwhile, fill a big pot with 2 litres of water and bring it to the boil. Add the dried apples, shiitake mushrooms, dates, radishes and kombu and leave to cook for 10 minutes.

4. Remove the pan from the heat and leave it to infuse. This is your stock.

5. Once the water has cooled, remove and discard the dried ingredients from the stock using a slotted spoon.

6. Scoop out a cupful of the stock and set aside to use later.

7. Stir the sweet rice powder into the rest of the stock until it takes on a sticky porridge-like consistency. Bring this mixture to boil, then remove it from the heat and let it cool down overnight – don't put it in the fridge. You should have about 1 litre of this sticky rice sauce.

8. The next day, tip the radishes into a colander over the sink to drain.

9. Wash the cabbages thoroughly and leave them to drain in a colander for about 1–2 hours.

10. Meanwhile, make the marinade. Put the garlic, onions, ginger and pears in a food processor with both lots of shrimps, pour in 100ml of your reserved stock and pulse until the mixture becomes a grainy paste.

11. Spoon the paste into a big bowl and stir in the fish sauce, dried red pepper flakes and the sticky rice sauce. Keep stirring while you add a bit more stock (or water) to loosen the mixture until it is the consistency of ketchup.

12. Finely chop the spring onions and chives to the size of your pinky finger and add these to the shrimp paste marinade.

13. Taste the marinade and add grog sol if it's not salty enough. If it tastes a bit saltier than a typical kimchi you like, it's perfect.

14. Add the washed cabbages to the bowl and rub the marinade into them evenly and thoroughly (you don't use the marinade for the radishes).

15. Now you can start filling the plastic containers to begin the fermentation process. Start with a layer of radishes, then add a layer of cabbages. Repeat, until each container is full.

16. The especially tough outer leaves from the cabbages can be placed over the top layer before sealing each container.

17. If the kimchi is left at room temperature, check it in a week. When it starts giving off a strong sour scent, it's fermented and ready to eat. If you keep it in the fridge, it will be perfectly fermented after one month.

Destination:
Jeju Island

The Sisterhood

자매애

Jamae-ae

Let's go Jeju!

Jeju Island is one of the most pristine islands in Korea and is madly popular with tourists. It lies in the Korea Strait, a one-hour flight from Seoul. A volcanic island with stunning beaches, lava cliffs and, up in the mountains, roaring waterfalls and bathing pools, it is called the Hawaii of Korea. In spring and summer, the island is covered with cherry blossom and bright pink and red azaleas in bloom. And then there are the Jeju lava tube caves, considered one of the most unique underground cave systems in the world. They were formed around 300,000 years ago when lava flowed from a volcano to the sea, creating a tube system that included caves. Some walls and roofs are covered in multi-coloured carbonate deposits, turning them into murals of swirling colours designed by mother nature.

I travelled to Jeju with my friend, Kyung-sook Shin, and immediately Jeju surprised me. I was expecting a small, remote island, but I found the capital, Jeju City, which we flew into, a thriving and growing urban metropolis. From there, we rented a car, and as we drove into the countryside, the high-rise office blocks and apartment buildings, restaurants, hotels and tourist attractions faded away. Now we were in the Jeju of my imagination, with grass the colour of emerald, fields of canola flowers and cherry blossom, and volcanic rock formations jutting out of the ocean. We passed women in cotton bonnets picking cucumbers and papayas. And every field was bordered by walls made from volcanic rock to protect the crops from the winds.

We arrived at a small hotel on the far side of the island, dropped our bags and took a walk through the village of tiny houses, painted in ice cream colours of strawberry pink, pistachio green and lemon yellow. Their small lawns were decorated with colourful tiles and seashells, a sign that the ocean is part of everyone's lives here. The locals on Jeju are outside most of the time, farming, working and playing. No one sits at home in front of their computers or televisions day and night. Nature is the best entertainment imaginable.

We strolled along a dirt path that led us to a small farm. The earth was a deep chocolate brown, and we leaned down to grab a handful. It was velvet to the touch. Jeju farmers lead the way in Korea with their organic farming methods, collectives and eco-friendly practices. Here, you won't find genetically modified and cloned tangerines, but natural fruits and vegetables grown under the sub-tropical sun.

We spied a bookstore in the little hamlet and went inside to see if they stocked any of Kyung-sook's books. To our delight, they did. Kyung-sook didn't want to make a fuss, but I proudly announced that the famous author was in the shop. Once again, I observed the grace and humility of my Korean friend. Like all Koreans I have come across, she is humble, would find it impossible to brag and is grateful for even the smallest kindness.

In every one of Kyung-sook's books she includes this frontispiece message to her readers: "It will honour me if you are kind to others, friends as well as strangers."

The mermaids of Korea

Jeju is famous for its female divers, *haenyeo*, literally "sea women". *Haenyeo* have been harvesting the ocean by hand since the seventeenth century. The most athletic women you will likely see in Korea, they are a remarkable sisterhood of free-divers who gather conch, sea cucumbers, abalone (sea snails) and sea urchins to sell at market. My motivation for visiting Jeju was to meet some of these extraordinary women to learn their secrets to longevity and happiness.

While driving along the shoreline of the island, we had spotted intriguing circular stone walls every few miles. They are known as *bulteok* and are the traditional dressing rooms of the *haenyeo*, who would use them as places to eat, collect and distribute their catch. We also saw the more modern, heated huts that they now use, painted with seascapes and portraits of themselves.

Haenyeo spend up to seven hours harvesting during the three months of the season. Wearing wetsuits, flippers and scuba masks and with lead weights around their waists to help them descend, they must plunge to depths of 5–20 metres. During each dive, they hold their breath for up to two minutes and when resurfacing, they make a unique whistling sound known as *sumbisori* to expel air from their lungs and let their team know they are returning to the surface and safe. Many *haenyeo* pray to sea gods before diving, asking for protection – from the sharks, jellyfish and storms – and a good catch.

The divers work as a team and a business collective – *jeong* in action! – sharing their catch equally, supporting each other in illness and sorrow, and celebrating together in joy.

Haenyeo prove that age is no barrier to doing what you love. The majority of them today are in their sixties, but I met some *haenyeo* in their eighties who told me they won't stop diving. They are a symbol of resilience like no other.

Korea's first working mothers

The first records of *haenyeo* diving for abalone date to 1629, so their understanding of the sea and marine life is, not just generations, but centuries deep. Two missionaries who travelled to Jeju in 1899 were so impressed by the *haenyeo* that they wrote:

"Women of [Jeju] might be called the Amazonians of Korea. They not only do all the work but greatly exceed the men in number; on the streets, one meets three women to one man. This is because so many men are away sailing. The women are more robust and much better looking than their sisters on the mainland."

The *haenyeo* began diving because their men were often lost at sea from fishing accidents or at war, and they were left to support their families. Wives took the place of their husbands doing this dangerous work, even diving while pregnant.

Later, with men enslaved by the Japanese and Chinese, women again were left alone to feed their families. A *haenyeo* told me that the male population had now increased on the island, but they were afraid to let men dive. They wanted to protect them because they were too precious.

Training

Haenyeo are divided into three groups according to level of experience: *hagun*, (lowest skilled), *junggun* (middle skilled) and *sanggun* (highest skilled). The *sanggun*, revered for their wisdom, offer guidance to others. Training begins as teenagers, and it takes about seven years to reach proficiency.

Haenyeo dive in teams, always watching out for each other. If a diver does not surface in time, the others will stop diving to rescue them.

The tragedy of *haenyeo* dying if they don't ascend is never far from their minds either. In the last decade, around 55 women have died while diving, the majority over the age of 70.

Role models

Today these iconic women have been designated by the provincial government as representatives of the island's character and people's spirit. Jeju's *haenyeo* have also contributed much to the advancement of women's status in the community, as well as promoting environmental sustainability with their eco-friendly methods and management of fishing practices. They respect the marine ecosystem, harvest only in season and take just enough to sustain their community. They explained that because they don't overfish, the ocean continues to provides all they need and asks for nothing in return.

For me, the *haenyeo* are such extraordinary examples of sisterhood, beauty and success. They live by the principles of *jeong* (we before me), *han* (grit in the face of difficulty) and *heung* (joy in nature).

I was honoured to meet with some of them, such dignified and powerful women who are not defined by men or society. They have made their own rules. And they rule!

No surprise, then, given their extraordinary lives and fearless personalities, that *haenyeo* have featured as characters in a number of K-dramas and K-movies. *My Mother the Mermaid* (2004) was about a mother who used to be a diver, while *Canola* (2016) has a *haenyeo* grandmother on Jeju dealing with her rebellious grand-daughter from Seoul.

Meet the mermaids

If you want to see the *haenyeo* in action while visiting Jeju Island, hike up to Sunrise Peak, Seongsan Ilchulbong. Formed more than 5000 years ago, it's a 182-metre (600-feet) volcano with a forested crater. Every day (at 1:30 pm and 3 pm) you can attend the Women Diver Show, where *haenyeo* sing traditional songs, dive and then share their catch with those in attendance.

After seeing them in person, head to the Haenyeo Museum. It's a profoundly moving experience to learn about their history, working lives and extraordinary co-existence with the ocean that continues to this day.

The most important issue the *haenyeo* face now is the disappearance of their culture. In 1965, over 23,000 *haenyeo* were diving. Today, there are an estimated 3500. Many of the divers say the tradition may not survive another generation since many of their daughters have decided to take jobs in the city. Their livelihood is at risk from the rising sea levels and the industrialisation of fishing, which makes free-diving for seafood unnecessary. Yet their culture of bravery, independence and persistence continues to inspire.

Women Diver Show
Address: 284-12 Ilchul-ro, Seongsan-eup, Seogwipo-si, Jeju-do

Haenyeo Museum
Address: 26, Haenyeobangmulgwan-gil, Gujwa-eup, Jeju-si, Jeju-do
Website: www.haenyeo.go.kr

The mermaid meal

One of my most memorable dining experiences was on Jeju Island, with Kyung-sook. Thanks to its crystal-clear waters, it's also where you will find the finest seafood.

One day during our visit, we were driving along the coast when Kyung-sook's phone rang. Given her serious tone, I assumed something was wrong. Suddenly she swung the car around sharply.

"We have to make it before it closes!"

I had no idea where we going but after a few miles she turned into an old building covered with graffiti and stopped the car.

"Hurry up! They close in a few minutes. This is the best seafood on the island!"

I followed as she hurried into the small restaurant filled with wobbly chairs, linoleum tables and plaster walls. Two women wearing printed head kerchiefs were covered in sweat cooking over a big wrought-iron stove.

We had just had a huge lunch. "I don't think I can eat anything else," I cried as we sat at a small table by the window.

"They close in half an hour, and we have to leave tomorrow. This is our only chance," Kyung-sook insisted.

Soon a hot plate was placed at the centre of our table without us even ordering. I learned there is only one meal served in the restaurant. An oversized pot of seafood stew filled with broth, crab, mussels, abalone, clams and fish arrived. The aroma rising from the pot conjured up the sea.

Despite being full, as I tasted the stew, my stomach felt empty again and I ate with gusto. We both did. Later the waitress mixed the leftover broth into a bowl of abalone porridge: rice, abalone and more seafood.

As I spooned the porridge into my mouth, a seaweed-tasting liquid sprayed onto my tongue. It was a sea squirt; a marine animal I was told produces a substance which has anti-cancer properties. The texture of the rice and silky smooth seaweed and marine broth was hands down the most fantastic meal I have ever eaten.

Once again, this meal was not just about food. It was about Jeju Island, and the pristine waters that were home to the sea animals and seaweed I was eating right then.

I will never forget this abalone porridge; and I have vowed to return to Jeju to eat it again.

Lessons in happiness from the Sisterhood

- *Haenyeo* are a shining example of *han* – and the satisfaction to be found in physical work or exercise. Put time and effort into training and practising whatever you do, from cooking to yoga, playing tennis or training your dog. *Haenyeo* training is long and arduous but pays off. Be like *Haenyeo* in all your endeavours. Never give up.
- *Haenyeo* are proof that the path to success is about teamwork. By practising mutual respect and caring for one another – the principle of *jeong* – we can create a more enriching and mutually beneficial community.
- Respect mother nature. *Haenyeo* co-exist with the ocean and have strict limits on fishing. Revere the earth and the ocean – help to preserve, restore and invigorate the planet because it will benefit us all.
- Travel with a friend. Share your travel dreams and wishes, even from your sofa. Shared dreams and memories are richer, fuller and more life sustaining.
- See ageing as a blessing. The best years can be ahead of you. *Haenyeo* still dive at 80! Learn to love yourself as you age and realises that you can find new adventures, excitement, love and passion as you grow older.

Squid Radish Soup

오징어무국

(Ohjinguh moogook)

There are hangover cures the world over, but this one from Kim Geoungmin might be the most unique.

"I've always loved squid, whether simply grilled with butter or pan-fried with onion, garlic, and spring onion.

"In this dish, the most important ingredient, apart from the obvious star, is the sesame oil, which adds this unique, irresistible aroma.

"This recipe is not a conventional one, and I asked my mom – who's a great cook – for her tips here and there. She has this reputation of being 'big-handed', which means she cooks everything party-sized for sharing. I did take after her a bit in that respect, so I tend to use a whole squid for my soup, but for people new to squid, I recommend using half or less. However, if you do end up making too much, no worries at all – this is great hangover food, and perfect as a big after-party breakfast for all your friends who ended up staying over."

Ingredients

(Serves 2)

1 handful dried anchovies

1 handful dried kombu kelp

Pinch of dried red pepper flakes (optional)

1 tbsp vegetable or sesame oil

1 squid, gutted and washed, chopped into bite-sized pieces

⅓ Korean radish, chopped into bite-sized pieces

½ spring onion

3 garlic cloves, crushed

2 tbsp Korean soy sauce

1 tsp salt

Pinch of black pepper

1. First you need to make your stock: fill a saucepan with 1.5 litres of water and bring it to the boil, then reduce the heat and add the dried anchovies, kombu kelp and a pinch of dried red pepper flakes, if you like a bit of spice.

2. Simmer the stock over a medium heat for 5–10 minutes, or until the liquid has turned the colour of pale beer. Don't leave it much longer or the kelp will turn gelatinous and make the stock a bit slimy. An alternative method is to soak all the ingredients in lukewarm water for an hour.

3. While the stock is simmering (or stewing), place a large saucepan over a high heat, pour in the oil and stir-fry the chopped squid and radish pieces.

4. Once the radish looks translucent and the squid has some red water seeping out, add 700ml stock and bring to the boil.

5. Stir the spring onion and crushed garlic into the soup and cook for a few more minutes, before seasoning with soy sauce, salt and pepper.

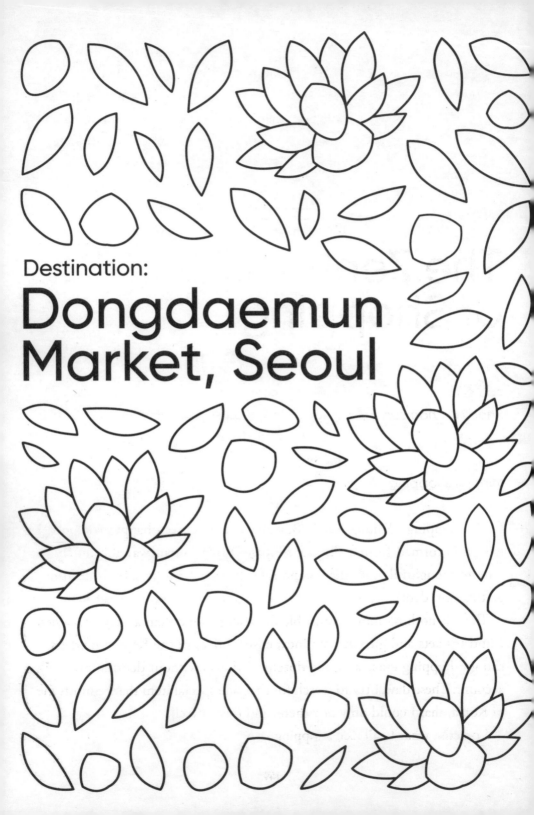

Destination:

Dongdaemun Market, Seoul

The Zen
of Shopping

쇼핑 참선
Shoping chamsun

<u>Mindful shopping</u>

I love shopping. Who doesn't? But over the years, I'm happy to report, I have transformed from a chronic shopaholic who spent way too much, to a more thoughtful, considerate and safe shopper (and by safe, I mean not getting into debt).

There is nothing more irresistible for a shopaholic than a bargain. When I find trinkets and gifts at such inexpensive prices in the Korean markets, I can go shopping crazy and buy dozens of things without denting my bank account. These days I try to search for that one special item that reminds me of Korea, that I could only buy there, and treat myself.

I practise what I call Zen shopping.

In Korean Zen, practitioners will meditate on a *hua tou*, a question or story. "What is this?" is one of the central questions to ask yourself in an attempt to achieve a more balanced, insightful self. Whereas I used to be intoxicated by shopping, buying clothes, shoes, gifts and "stuff" I didn't need, now, I can look at something and ask, "What is this?"

Shopping for me today includes looking, window-shopping, trying on clothes, asking myself questions and considering the cost. Is that simple linen blouse really worth US$400? Is that yarn worth US$250 a skein? What is this pair of US$500 shoes with high heels? Are they comfortable? Will I wear them? Why do I want them?

This more mindful practice of shopping has saved me from debt and despair.

But while I practice mindful shopping, there is one place in the world where I still indulge in shopping madness, and that's Seoul!

I have learned to experience *heung* – the greatest joy – when I walk through the traditional Korean markets amidst miles of wondrous fabrics, bags, pants, shirts, housewares, jewellery and more. Here, the most precious items are the special bargains and simple things I've found, like plastic pinkie rings in every colour for US$2.00, a gift to twenty girlfriends back home. Or a pair of bronze patent-leather shoes for US$30 that looked just like Prada!

Shopping in Korea isn't about the amount of money you spend; it's about the unique style you will find nowhere else. It's K-pop fashion meets designer and vintage, all worn by young and old alike. Best of all, it feels like a big treasure hunt.

The great treasure hunt

I was on a visit to Seoul for the book fair with my Italian friend and co-agent, Gabriella. She wanted to visit a traditional market during our stay, which truthfully sounded dull to me. I was thinking it would be cheesy replicas of ancient objects and old-fashioned goods. But Gabriella said we must go because a local market is a wonderful opportunity to imbibe the culture and meet the local people.

So along with another colleague, off we went to Dongdaemun Market near the Dongdaemun Gate, one of the eight old city gates, now in the middle of Seoul. The market is surrounded by highways, and to get to the entrance I had to dodge, duck and dive between the endless cars, motorbikes and trucks zipping by. Made up of 26 shopping malls, 30,000 speciality shops and 50,000 manufacturers, the market covers more than ten blocks; it's a wholesale and retail shopping paradise in one.

We entered the market, our eyes as wide as the moon. All we could do was shake our heads, laugh and say, "Unbelievable! Unbelievable!"

Twenty-four hours a day, you can buy anything there from ribbons, toasters, fabrics, toys, clothes, electronics, shoes – you name it! The variety is astonishing, and the prices so low that will have to buy a suitcase to take all your purchases home – as I did. And when I went to find one, there wasn't just one store, but an entire floor of suitcases to choose from.

Looking for gifts for family and friends, we bought fans, embroidered silk purses and costume jewellery. I love knitting, and was thrilled to find Korean yarn, *dodam*, made from traditional *hanji* paper and best suited for crafting bags and hats.

We kept moving up and down the aisles. Suddenly, my eye was caught by a sign in a tailor's shop window advertising dresses custom-made within 24 hours. I went in and met a lovely tailor who explained that if I bought the fabric, he could indeed make a dress in a day. Now I had a real mission! I had written a novel, *The J.M. Barrie Ladies Swimming Society*, which had been translated into Korean and was being published in Seoul that week. I needed a dress for the press conferences and the book's launch party. It was all so terribly exciting!

We plunged into the fabric market, and I went digging through what felt like thousands of bolts of material, my eyes darting from colour to colour, from stripes to flowers and polka dots until I found a beautiful blue silk with tiny sailboats that looked very French. I bought the fabric for less than US$30 and sped back to the tailor with it in hand. We huddled in his tiny shop, where he took my measurements and I draped the fabric over myself while my friends suggested ideas. I ordered one shirt dress and one A-line. They cost about US$100 to design and sew overnight.

Would you believe at 9am the next day the dresses were ready, each fitting perfectly.

That day, I bought a beautiful dress and also made a friend. Now whenever I am in Seoul, I return to the market and have a dress or shirt made by the kind tailor.

Dongdaemun Market is also heaven for street food lovers. After shopping, and to celebrate our purchases, I like to eat *japchae* (noodles) and vegetable pancakes at a tiny food bar, squeezed in with my friends like sardines.

Another Seoul market worth your time – also famous for its street food – is Gwangjang Market, where you can find beautiful fabrics and textiles along with traditional items and clothing for Korean rituals. Make sure to go with an empty stomach so you can try the famous *nokdu-jeon*, (mung bean pancake), and *mayak gimbap*, (seaweed rice roll). Know that *mayak* actually means "drug" because the rice rolls are so addictive, they make you return for more!

Dongdaemun Market
Address: 18-221 Euljiro 6(yuk)-ga, Jung-gu, Seoul
Website: www.ddm-mall.co.kr

Gwangjang Market
Address: 88 Changgyeonggung-ro, Jongno-gu, Seoul
Website: www.kwangjangmarket.co.kr/en/

Elder cool

Dressing fashionably and creatively is for people of all ages. And in Seoul, it is common to see older people wearing the hippest, most original looks they have created themselves. Rules dictating what a 70-year-old should wear in London or New York don't apply there. Just like the *haenyeo* still diving at 80, Koreans embrace every year of their lives.

Kim Dong-hyun is an up-and-coming fashion photographer who shoots street fashion in Seoul. His speciality is capturing the style of senior Korean fashionistas, who tend to congregate and shop at Dongmyo flea market near Dongmyo train station. He has immortalised their unique style, which ranges from military to denim and vintage luxury brands, in a book called *Mut: Street Fashion of Seoul.* ("Mut" refers to the Korean word *meot*, which means cool or fabulous.)

I love that he wants people of all ages to celebrate their style, be it vintage, modern or a mish-mash of the two. As he says, "Clothes are a great pleasure for everyone."

Hanbok heritage

The beautiful *hanbok* was the standard dress of Koreans for several hundred years before the country opened up to the world. Consisting of *jeogori* (jacket), *chima* (billowing skirt) or *baji* (trousers), the *hanbok* is typically made of silk, ramie or cotton in vivid colours.

While Koreans today wear Western dress, they still don *hanbok* for special occasions like holidays, weddings and funerals. This respect for and connection to the past through dress is an example of *han, heung* and *jeong*. In fact, Korea's Cultural Heritage Administration designated the wearing of *hanbok* as "national intangible cultural heritage".

Recently, Jane Seymour, the international screen and TV star, wore a magnificent *hanbok* to her son's wedding to honour her Korean daughter-in-law. I also love that today the *hanbok* is experiencing a resurgence beyond just ritual use. It was the Korean fashion industry that first rediscovered it as inspiration, particularly designer Lee Young-hee, who showcased restyled *hanbok* silhouettes on the Paris catwalks in the 1990s.

Today, designers Kim Young-jin and Leesle Hwang make contemporary iterations of *hanbok*–glamour for evening, cropped jackets and skirts for day, using non-traditional fabrics, giving the younger generation a modern link to their history. But maybe the biggest drivers of the modern *hanbok* movement are the K-pop phenomenons BTS and Blackpink. When they started wearing them, the craze was official!

You can shop for traditional *hanbok* in Gwangjang Market, but you can also wear looks from today's runways – Korean designers now show twice a year at Seoul Fashion Week. And like everything *hallyu*, Korean designers are also gaining steam outside the country.

Korean streetwear brand Juun J now shows at Paris Fashion Week. Unisex Korean brand Heich Es Heich is popular among K-pop artists. Designer Minju Kim earned global recognition after winning the Netflix "Next in Fashion" contest with her oversize silhouettes and bold patterns. It's definitely time to put some Korean style in your wardrobe. Here's a list of brands to look out for:

Leesle Hwang
Website: www.leesle.kr

Kim Young-jin
Website: www.tchaikim.co.kr

Juun J.
Website: www.juunj.com

Heich Es Heich
Website: www.heich.kr

Minjukim
Website: www.minjukim.co

Newtro – Korean vintage

One of the most interesting trends in Korean fashion and shopping is "newtro" or new retro. Some have described it as Korea's version of hipster culture, but I think the movement is profound and follows the Korean way of incorporating history, politics and social issues into cultural practices, including what to wear.

Newtro has Koreans born in the 1980s and 1990s embracing looks from as far back as the nineteenth century through to the decades when they were born. Some of the movement is driven by nostalgia for retro fashion, and by social media and TV shows such as the period dramas *Mr Sunshine,* (set in the nineteenth century) and *Pachinko*. But underpinning newtro is a generational push to address climate change and economic challenges by living and dressing more sustainably.

Now vintage and thrift stores in Seoul are full of shoppers, both young and old, making a political statement through purchasing affordable, beautiful, pre-loved fashion. What better way to help the environment and your wallet? I can't think of a more inspiring fashion trend than that!

The couple look

One other curious trend in Korea when it comes to fashion trends is the "couple look". Young couples shop for matching outfits and wear them to show off and celebrate their relationship. It could be just simple basics, such as T-shirts in complementary colours, or they can go all-out and buy pre-designed "his and hers" whole outfits.

The practice can be traced back to the post-war years when Korean couples dressed similarly on their honeymoon as a way to show everyone they were, well, on their honeymoon. But recently it has really taken off with couples in earlier stages of their relationship adopting the style, largely due to social media.

I have seen many couples in matching outfits in Seoul, and while at first glance it might look like another fashion fad, in Korea it has real resonance. In a culture that is so focused on marriage and family, people gain social currency when they're in a relationship, and the "couple look" is an easy way to signal their status and any relationship milestone.

Now madly popular on Instagram (search for #couplelook), this is one trend that isn't just about loving clothes, but love and clothes.

Ready, set, go!

To see Olympic-medal-level shoppers in action, head to the neighbourhood of Myeongdong. One of Seoul's shopping meccas, it's probably the most popular in Korea among both locals and tourists, with an estimated 1 million people visiting every day. There are hundreds of shops, restaurants and designer stores here, from fast fashion H&M and Zara to luxury department stores Shinsegae and Lotte. The energy is non-stop electricity on the streets, and below them too, since Myeongdong has a huge underground shopping centre. It is a maze of alleys filled with small stalls and shopfronts connected to the big department stores. Here, I found shirts and dresses made of the finest linen from Vietnam that are perfect for the hot summer months, in colours and textures I had not seen anywhere else. The prices were one tenth of what I would pay in New York.

And if you don't want to stop shopping to sit down for a meal, Myeongdong has street food carts everywhere. Try the Tornado Potato or the Korean Fried Chicken. The other thing to do while giving your credit card a break is to watch the Dragon Beard candy-makers. They rap while they spin honey and cornstarch into fine-haired threads of candy for you:

You from New York – ah ah ah New York
This is hard – honey very very hard
You know King Dragon Beard King
Honey rock hard honey.

It was pure theatre and the best entertainment I'd seen in Seoul.

Your perfect complexion

Myeongdong is also ground zero for K-beauty offerings, which as you already know (see Chapter 7) have taken over the world. It has the most skincare stores and cosmetic shops in Korea – along the main strip they sit bumper to bumper, often twenty in a single block! Every great Korean brand, including Innisfree, Sulwhasoo and Laneige, is here, all offering face creams, serums, masks and face skins (paper masks soaked in lotion). There are also some unique products on offer that you must try. Don't be shy!

I discovered salmon egg sleeping masks (for skin clarifying) and snail mucin cream (made from black snails), a wonderful moisturiser. (After you purchase anything you will be given free samples, which is a great way to try new products.)

I also found a fascinating store selling only products made from charcoal: charcoal tea, masks and face creams. I couldn't imagine smearing it on my face, but I was in Korea, the land of eternal beauty, so I asked the shop-keeper, "So what's as the secret about charcoal?"

I was told that activated charcoal is a fine black powder that's produced when common charcoal is exposed to high heat. This makes it highly absorbent and able to trap chemicals and toxins, so very effective in skincare products. It is said to help tighten skin – no Botox needed for me! I was going to try some charcoal cream! Why not? It also brightens your teeth, which is why I bought twenty tubes of charcoal toothpaste.

A world unto itself

Looking for the ultimate department store in Korea? My advice is to go straight to Lotte. The main branch is in Myeongdong. Lotte is Disneyland for shoppers who have money to burn. It's the place to drown in luxury – the Bergdorf Goodman of Korea, only chicer! So, go indulge and enjoy it, but don't forget your passport. Lotte, along with other big stores, and offers tax-free purchases to foreigners for any purchase between 30,000–500,000 Korean won.

Lotte Department Store
Address: 81, Namdaemun-ro, Jung-gu, Seoul
Website: www.lotte.co.kr

Insa-dong buzz

Insa-dong is one of my favourite spots in Seoul, filled with small antique and vintage clothing shops, wooden tea houses and bookstores along its narrow alleyways. Art galleries here specialise in traditional Korean art and ceramics.

I love the tiny boutiques operated by young budding designers, some of whom sew their own clothes right there in the store. It's like the Greenwich Village of Seoul.

Insadong Shopping
Address: 62, Insadong-gil, Jongno-gu, Seoul
Website: www.insainfo.or.kr

Shop "Gangnam Style"

In 2012, one pop song took over the world: "Gangnam Style". With its catchy beat and "horse galloping" dance moves, the music video went viral – it was the first to reach more than a billion views on YouTube. (Today it is more than 4 billion!) Yet what made it truly earth shattering was that it was sung not by a pop star from the West, but by the Korean rapper and songwriter Psy (Park Jae-sang).

The song, satirising the citizens of the uber-wealthy Seoul suburb of Gangnam, turned Psy into a global superstar and attracted millions to attend his concerts.

Now you know the song, shop the neighbourhood!

Gangnam is the most exclusive shopping area in Seoul. Think Fifth Avenue in New York City, Rodeo Drive in Beverly Hills, Bond Street in London or rue du Fabourg Saint-Honoré in Paris.

The hottest Korean luxury brand, MCM, has its flagship store in Gangnam, and it's totally worth a visit to shop its famous leather goods and hip clothes beloved of celebrities and K-pop stars.

MCM is more than just a successful business, it's also a powerful symbol of the Korean traits of grit and perseverance that make up *han*. MCM has put Korean luxury on the map, and it's thanks to one woman.

The owner and chairperson of the global fashion empire, Sung-Joo Kim, was the youngest of four boys and three girls, born into one of Korea's richest families. Her strict Confucian father left everything to the men in the family, and after refusing an arranged marriage, Sung-Joo was disinherited. She went to New York and worked at Bloomingdales to learn the fashion business, then returned to Korea in 1990 to go where few women had gone before: into business, distributing European luxury brands. With a small loan, she used her brains, creativity and persistence to buy MCM in 2005 and turned it into a monster success.

Step into the store and you will think you are in a museum, with its Bauhaus-inspired interiors and raw concrete walls and floors. In fact, it does include an art gallery – Konig Galerie – on the fifth floor. Here's a tip: don't bring a cup of coffee into the shop – you'll be stopped at the door!

Another good place for fashionistas when looking for luxury brand shoes and clothes is the Galleria Department Store; also Garosu-gil, the famous tree-lined street that is home to Korean brands, galleries and hip boutiques.

But for me the real star of Gangnam is the Starfield COEX Mall, Asia's largest underground shopping mall. Outside the entrance is a giant Gangnam Style bronze sculpture of two overlapping hands in the style of the song's "horsey" dance, to celebrate Psy putting the area on the map.

If movie theatres, shopping, food, an aquarium and a casino are not enough, you can visit the incredible Starfield Library, which holds 50,000 books and magazines. Book lovers from all over the world make pilgrimages here to soak up the atmosphere, attend cultural events and yes, take pictures for their social media.

The mall is beneath the COEX exhibition complex, and whenever I go to the Seoul Book Fair, I nip downstairs during a break and shop. The centre is a maze and I have gotten lost more than once, so check the mall map!

And finally, it's worth taking a break from shopping for handbags to learn about their history and see the craftsmanship put into them at the Simone

Handbag Museum. An entire museum dedicated to fashionable Western handbags from 1550 to the present day – from French attachable linen pockets to 21st-century "it" bags. The 300 bags on exhibit invite you to look at the changing fashion cycles and how handbags speak to women's identities. It's located inside a building that looks like a bag, so you can't miss it!

MCM
Address: 412 Apgujeong-ro
Cheongdam-dong, Gangnam-gu, Seoul
Website: www.mcmworldwide.com

Galleria Department Store
Address: 343 Apgujeong-ro, Gangnam-gu, Seoul
Website: www.dept.galleria.co.kr/en

Starfield COEX Mall
Address: 513, Yeongdong-daero, Gangnam-gu, Seoul
Website: www.starfield.co.kr

Simone Handbag Museum
17 Dosan-Daero 13 Gil (Sinsa-Dong), Gangnam-gu, Seoul
Website: www.simonehandbagmuseum.co.kr

Need to know

One important lesson I learned when shopping in Korea: Korean women only wear flat shoes – I have never seen them in high heels. After buying a pair of flats, my feet told me never to wear heels again. Another secret to Korean happiness! Shopping in Seoul taught me what feels good and looks good from the inside out. I now try to follow the Korean fashion precepts of practical, elegant, simple and casual chic.

Lessons from shopping in Korea

- Shopping is a great way to explore. Visit different areas of a city or village to find its best-kept local secrets.
- Always shop the traditional markets – that is where you will see the real Korea and bargains you won't believe.
- Be adventurous with your skincare products. Try seahorse cream and black snail facials.
- Shop for local designs and styles because you won't find them anywhere else. Don't be afraid to wear something different and new.
- You can dress fashionably and creatively at any age. Clothes should be a pleasure for everyone.
- Try to buy vintage and second-hand when you can – not only is it more fun to hunt for hidden, one-off treasures; it is more environmentally friendly.

My associate Sue Park loved rice burgers when living in Korea. But after moving to the US, she couldn't find them as easily, and had to improvise.

"When my friends and I were at school in Korea, rice burgers were one of our go-to snacks.

"Koreans have this notion of *babshim*, which literally translates as 'power of steamed rice'. And yes, we do believe that we can go about our everyday, professional and social life smoothly only when our belly is full of steamed rice. So it's no surprise that we try to incorporate steamed rice – if impossible, something made of rice at least – into everything, and burgers were not an exception. Rice burgers also feel in a way like a Western version of Korean *kimbap* (rice rolls) or *jumeokbap* (rice balls), so they became an instant hit across the country as a cousin to these popular rice snacks and as a gluten-free, healthier alternative to classic Western burgers.

"But when I moved to the US, I couldn't just casually walk into a cafeteria or diner and order a rice burger. When I was studying away from home and trying out various recipes myself, I also realised that American rice grains are surprisingly different from the Korean ones – because of their different texture and consistency, they don't make the kind of rice buns I would like for my burger. They wouldn't stick together, and the buns always ended up too sticky or crumbled apart as soon as I tried to lift them.

"So I resorted to making *bapjeon* (rice pancake) instead – a combination of a classic omelette and steamed rice – and ate it with side dishes that I would have normally put between my rice buns. Then it hit me – I could just use these rice pancakes as buns instead! A simple eureka, really, but it proved to be the easiest and quickest way to make steamy, delicious rice buns that are still full of color and protein."

Ingredients

(Serves 1)

2 eggs
1 tsp curry powder
1 tsp maple syrup
½ tsp salt
2 tsp parsley and dill,
chopped finely
150g steamed sushi rice,
left to cool (ideally it
should be leftovers from
the day before)
1 tbsp cooking oil
100g or more minced
beef (depending on how
much meat you want)
¼ small onion, finely
chopped

Toppings

4 or more pickles
3 or more leaves of
cabbage or lettuce
Condiments of your
choosing

1. Beat two eggs in a bowl and add the curry powder, maple syrup, a pinch of salt and half the parsley and dill.

2. Stir the cooked rice into the seasoned eggs. If the mixture seems too runny, add some more rice. You can also add a teaspoon of softened butter or olive oil at this stage to give it a richer taste.

3. Heat a small frying pan, add some cooking oil and spoon half the mixture into the pan. Cook until it's nicely browned, before flipping it over with a spatula to cook on the other side. Leave it a bit longer if you like it crispy around the edges. Remove from the pan and set aside while you cook the other half of the mixture.

4. In a bowl, make the burger by mixing the minced beef, chopped onion, the remaining parsley and dill and a little seasoning. Shape the mixture into a patty in your hands.

5. Heat the pan again and fry your burger for a few minutes on both sides.

6. Now assemble your rice burgers, in the same way you'd make a regular burger, piling the patty, pickles and fresh greens between your rice buns, with any condiments of your choosing.

7. It's a good idea to eat it with a knife and fork as it won't be as easy to manage as a regular burger!

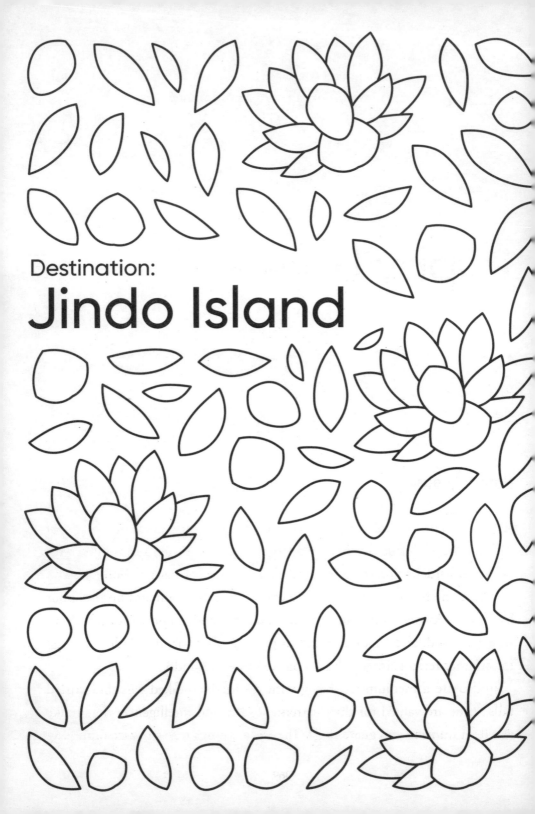

Destination:
Jindo Island

Puppy Love

애견

Aegyeon

National treasure

Jindo is a sub-tropical volcanic island that sits just off the southern tip of the Korean peninsula. It's the third-largest island in Korea and is filled with beautiful gardens, forests, waterfalls, caves, and other natural wonders. You can get there from Seoul by bus or a combination of train and bus in about five hours. As well as its stunning beauty, the island is known for its exceptional seafood, and I look forward to trying it! But for me, Jindo is special for another reason altogether – its native dogs: the Jindo.

Jindos are a medium-sized dog with distinctive perked ears and curled tails. They are valued for their extreme loyalty and intelligence; they make excellent hunting and guard dogs. There is a famous true story exemplifying

Jindos' loyalty. Baekgu, a female Jindo, born and raised on the island, was sold by her owner to someone in the city of Daejeon, only to show up seven months later tired and scruffy, having made the 180-mile journey home. Baekgu became a national star and was featured in children's books and cartoons. She even had a statue built in her honour.

Jindos are now considered one of Korea's national treasures and a symbol of friendship. To show the world how beloved they are, Korea had Jindos march in the opening ceremony of the 1988 Summer Olympic Games in Seoul.

In 2018, the North Korean leader Kim Jong-un gave former Korean President Moon Jae-in a pair of of white Pungsan dogs (relatives to the Jindo, hailing from the Kaema highlands of North Korea) in a show of cooperation and peace between the two countries. Decades earlier, his father had given two of these dogs to a previous South Korean president. The one-year-old dogs were handed over at the DMZ and lived in President Moon's residence for some years before being moved to Seoul Zoo.

Jindo dogs are not only symbolic; they also provide a livelihood for many local families who breed them on the island. It is estimated that between 30,000 and 50,000 puppies are bred annually and they cannot be taken off the island without a government permit.

There is no one explanation for how the Jindo came to Korea. Some say they were left behind after a Mongol invasion in the thirteenth century; others suggest they were bred by the royal family during the Joseon dynasty for guarding and hunting game.

As the spiritual and literal home of the Jindo, the island is the location for the headquarters of the Jindo Dog Project Office. This comprises a research centre and breeding facility, as well as a Jindo theme park and museum, where you can spend the day with the dogs, watch them perform feats of agility with their handlers and learn about their history.

Dogs are now the most popular pet in Korea, with an estimated 6 million living their best lives with human families. There seem to be no limits on how Korean dog owners will spoil their "babies" either, from designer dog clothes to dressing them in dog-sized traditional *hanbok* for Lunar New Year's Day, Seollal.

Whether it's a dog, cat or goldfish, I think pets are really important to our happiness because they connect us intimately with another living being. Owning a dog offers you unconditional love and companionship, lowers anxiety, gives you a reason to exercise daily, a chance to make new friends, and maybe even meet a partner!

Jindo Theme Park
Address: 57 Dongoe-ri, Jindo-eup, Jindo, Jeollanam-do
Website: www.jindo.go.kr

My best friend

I think I was born loving dogs, and I have always had a dog in my life since I was a child. My dogs have been my best friends, giving me unbridled joy and love, understanding, comfort and a sense of bonding that is greater than I have with any human. Even my husband knows that our dog, Lexi, comes first – and he has had to accept it!

I think every dog has a Korean soul. They exude the *heung, jeong* and *han* philosophies: they are full of exuberance and joy, bond with us like no other animal and they have the ability to withstand adversity. Dogs are my constant reminder and example of how to live.

Yet having a canine companion brings more than just joy. My dogs have given me profound solace during some very emotionally difficult experiences in my life. When my husband needed a liver transplant twelve years ago, I had to organise an emergency flight for him at 1am. My two white Labs, Futuro and Gala, lay close to my desk where I was making the arrangements, not leaving my side until everything was arranged; they understood. Their love truly gave me superhuman strength to complete my task.

Dogs come first

One of the most valuable lessons I learned about dogs and myself was while working in Korea.

Some years back, one of my beloved dogs had died. I was left bereft and trying to fill the emptiness in my heart. As the *Peanuts* cartoonist Charles M. Schulz famously said, "happiness is a warm puppy", and I couldn't agree more!

I had seen pictures of Jindo puppies and became fixated on getting one. They looked just like my dog who had died. I thought I could replace him by buying a Jindo dog – and, at the same time, I would be getting a piece of Korea too.

The next time I was in the country, I met with the Minister of Culture. He asked me how I would like the government to help me in relation to my book business. I blurted out, "I want a Jindo puppy!"

He was astounded and started laughing. But he promised to get me a Jindo to take back to New York; and, incredibly, he did. However, there was no time to fly to Jindo Island to pick him up as I was leaving shortly. Furthermore, a good friend in Seoul warned me against taking Jindo dogs out of their natural habitat.

I was out of luck in my dog quest. But I had also used the opportunity of my meeting with the Minister to bring up an uncomfortable topic – the Korean tradition of eating dog meat. Although demand for it has apparently diminished, nearly 1 million dogs are slaughtered for food every year in Korea. I had just sold Hwang Sun-mi's beautiful book, *The Dog Who Dared to Dream*, about the relationship between dog and man. I felt inspired to insist that the farming and butchering of man's best friend should be outlawed. The Minister assured me that Koreans love their dogs, and although some dog meat markets still remained, they were illegal. However, the consumption of dog meat is not.

It's encouraging to see how the tide is turning in favour of animal rights in Korea. In 2017, former President Moon Jae-in adopted a dog called "Tori", who had been rescued from a dog meat farm by an animal shelter. He has called for a ban on dog meat, as well as new measures to protect animal welfare and encourage pet adoption.

Kim Keon-hee, the current First Lady of Korea and a devoted dog owner has also called for the consumption of dog meat to be banned. It was considered a controversial step for the new First Lady, but I applaud her and hope a law will be introduced.

Many other politicians are following suit. It would be a vote winner with younger generations in Korea. My fervent wish is that the dog meat trade in Korea ends as soon as possible – like today! (Want to know what you can do? Write to the Humane Society International/Korea and the Korean government to press for a ban on dog meat. Join the movement here: www.hsi.org.)

Despite failing the first time, my quest for a Jindo puppy did not stop. Soon a friend's sister who worked for a dog rescue in Seoul said she could find me a Jindo puppy. Within a few days, she found me a beautiful Jindo whom I named Lucky. With an upcoming trip in the diary, I now set about making arrangements to bring Lucky back. I said nothing to my husband until we were on the way to the airport. Then I surprised him with the news. This was not a good idea.

He was not ready for another dog. Immediately, I went into damage control, and after apologising to everyone at the rescue centre, set about finding a home for Lucky.

At a dinner with the esteemed writer J.M. Lee, all I could do was cry about Lucky. Being the most kind and generous man, he said he would take care of him at his apple orchard. Then Kyung-sook Shin told me she had found a home for him with her brother in the countryside. She scolded me, and I felt so dreadful and selfish. She was right. My idea to take a Jindo dog to live in a New York apartment thousands of miles away would have backfired.

Lucky, a pure bred, belonged in Korea. The persona of the Jindo is so strong, it would have ruined the dog's life. (In fact, it is illegal to take a pure-bred Jindo out of Korea).

Today Lucky is a very happy dog in his new countryside home, while I have gained the most valuable insights from my mistake. Attempting to control the natural world, animal or plant, is neither wise, nor kind. The Korean way of seeking harmony in all things meant Lucky was not to become a New York dog. And that was the right outcome for Lucky.

The power of fables

So far, I've never had the time to visit Jindo Island, but I still dream about going there and plan to do so on my next trip. Meanwhile, I imagine what my visit will be like, and I believe it will go something like this.

First, I will visit a Jindo breeder, then another, and another, where I plan to be smothered by kisses from so many Jindo puppies I won't be able to count them all. I will take thousands of photos and fill myself up with Jindo puppiness until I leave.

While on the island, joyfully immersed in dog culture, I will bring a collection of Korean fables with me to read. Korean fables are a unique genre of literature enjoyed by children and adults. Typically featuring animals, they exemplify the philosophies of *han, heung* and *jeong* and are full of lessons about the complexities of life and how to navigate them.

There are literally hundreds of Korean fables about animals and nature: rocks that want to become whales and swim off into the ocean; a bird-shaped wind chime that becomes animated and flies round the world; the salmon whose silver scales mark him out as different – and dares to swim upstream beyond his fate.

The first fable I discovered was on my first trip to Korea – *The Hen Who Dreamed She Could Fly* by Sun-mi Hwang. It's the story of Sprout, a plucky little hen who leaves the hen house in search of her freedom and to end the tyranny of laying eggs that are always taken from her. She yearns to be a mother. After meeting a duck called Straggler, she finds an egg and sits on it, until a baby duck is born. Together they nurture the duck and protect it from a weasel. In the end, Sprout accepts the baby duck needs to fly away and fulfil its destiny. Sprout learns about the cycle of life, but also sacrifices herself to the weasel.

Sprout's experience reflects the three key Korean tenets of *han*, *heung* and *jeong*: *han* through the pain and suffering of losing her eggs; *heung* through the joy of being a mother; and *jeong* through the sense of being part of the whole barnyard community, which include the weasel and his babies.

In Sun-mi Hwang's next book, *The Dog Who Dared To Dream*, a dog named Scraggly lives a difficult life, breeding puppies for her owner. Each time her litter is sold, she is bereft. Yet Scraggly is so loyal to her owner that finally, in her old age, he comes to love her and appreciate her sacrifice.

Like other fables, this one exemplifies the Korean ethos of remaining loyal to family, friends and community through hardships, and attempting to find the joy in the simple pleasures of life.

In the West, we try to shield young people from pain and suffering. Social media, the internet and TV are escapes for them, and indeed for adults, from real life. But in Korea people understand that sadness and hardship are as much part of life as joy and happiness, and teach children that embracing them builds strength and character. I love the magic of these powerful stories of animals meeting their own challenges, in which we see ourselves and our own experiences.

The parting of the waters

Want to witness a Biblical miracle? Then head to Jindo, where a spectacular, natural phenomenon happens every spring. For about an hour, twice a day, the sea opens up to reveal a vast stretch of sand leading to nearby Modo Island. You can walk this path along the sea bed. Sound familiar? No wonder it's called the "Moses Miracle".

It is caused by tidal movements generating high and low tides – rather than the waters parting, it is in fact a lowering of the entire sea to reveal this piece of land. Before science, this natural phenomenon was explained by a folktale. According to local legend, Jindo was once inhabited by tigers, and when they started threatening the inhabitants, the locals fled to nearby Modo Island. But one woman named Bbyong was left behind. After praying to the *yongwang*, the local ocean god, Bbyong was told in a dream that a pathway made of a rainbow would appear in the sea so she could cross it. The next morning the sea parted and she returned to her family.

Today, every year, around 1 million people visit Jindo Island to walk the sea "road", take photos and dig for clams. It is such an event that it has its own festival – the Jindo Miracle Sea Road Festival, with an opening ceremony, concerts and street performers.

Jindo Miracle Sea Road Festival
Area of Modo-ri, Jindo-gun, Jeollanam-do
Website: www.jindo.go.kr/eng/main.cs

Lessons from Jindo Island

- Adopt a dog – a local one! They really are man's best friend. They will give you unconditional love, which you will return. They will force you to exercise, be outside in nature every day and get away from your problems during "dog play time". This is a gift.
- Respect a dog's breeding, and never move them to an environment that is not natural for them.
- Dogs are pure joy – *heung* – every day. Studies have shown that interacting with animals boosts your mood and decreases stress. Remember that even when they are barking at the post-man and need to be walked at 6am in the rain.
- Animals live in the moment and can inspire us to do the same.

This is a recipe for a traditional Korean dessert, which was given to me by Seong-ok Jang. Back in the day, it was usually made and sold by a local distillery, as a way of using up leftover alcohol. In that sense, this dessert follows the Korean tenet of "no edible going to waste".

In Western countries, this may seem like an odd way of making bread. But steaming is a technique that's existed for a very long time and is commonly practised in Korea. It produces a bread that is soft, moist and spongy.

"Since I bake for a living and am currently preparing to open up my own bakery, I tend to resort to the simplest route when it comes to cooking for myself.

"For snacks, I go for readily available recipes that make

use of an air fryer. Most of my Korean friends in their twenties and early thirties are the same – they always prefer to use short recipes they can find online, usually ones by Baek – the celebrity Korean chef who is a strong advocate of fast, modern-style cooking.

"So it's extremely rare, I'd say, for a young Korean to have an original recipe – or family recipe, for that matter – to bake. Especially because popular desserts in Korea today are from the West, and accordingly, the bakery I'm launching also sells largely Western desserts and sweets. But I'm also one of the lucky few who has a mother who likes to cook traditional Korean desserts. She graciously shared this barley alcohol bread recipe with me.

"The bread is traditionally made from a brewery's leftover barley, so people used to go to a local brewery, instead of a bakery, to get it. The garnishes vary depending on the baker's recipe, so you'll find many different toppings – toasted walnuts and sesame seeds, dried dates or pine nuts – anything that has a nutty, sweet flavour makes a wonderful accompaniment."

Ingredients

Serves 2–3

125g Korean rice wine (makgeolli)
150ml water
300g barley flour

Equipment

Individual muffin/ cupcake moulds or cake tin (not plastic)

Parchment paper

Bamboo steamer (worth purchasing if you don't already own one. Affordable, durable and versatile)

Toppings

6–10 glazed kidney beans
6–10 glazed green beans
6–10 glazed red beans
(You can buy these at Asian stores. Alternatively, use:)
1 dried date, sliced
1 dried persimmon, sliced
1 tsp sesame seeds, toasted
1 tbsp pine nuts or walnuts

1. Line your moulds with parchment paper. You can use cupcake moulds if you want to make individual bread rolls or a cake tin if you'd rather make a loaf. You shouldn't place the dough directly in the steamer as you want the loaf/ rolls to keep their shape and not stick together.

2. Pour the rice wine and water into a bowl and stir in the barley flour to form a dough.

3. Spoon the dough into the moulds, and scatter the toppings over each one.

4. Place the moulds inside the steamer.

5. Take a large pot and pour in enough water so it is one-third full. Put the pan on the hob and bring it to the boil. Place the steamer on top and close the lid.

6. Cook over a medium heat for about 25 minutes.

7. Turn off the heat and take care not to burn yourself on the hot steam as you take off the lid. The bread is cooked if you can insert a skewer or knife into it and it comes away clean.

8. This bread goes well with traditional Korean rice punch, which in spite of its name is non-alcoholic.

Conclusion: Perfect Happiness

완전한 행복

Wanjeonhan haengbok

What is perfect happiness? Is there such a thing? How do we attempt to achieve it? After all my years of Korean adventures and learning about the Korean mindset and national character, I think I may be on my way to unlocking the mystery.

In You-Jeong Jeong's international bestselling thriller, *Perfect Happiness*, the philosophy of the protagonist is simple. She decides to purge anything in her life that makes her unhappy. It just so happens that those obstacles of unhappiness include multiple husbands. She kills each of them and anyone else who gets in the way of her happiness. Now, I'm not advocating murder to find happiness – there are peaceful ways instead!

Aside from being a terrific read, the book made me think a great deal about the difference between Korean and Western ideas of happiness. In order to achieve happiness in the West, we try to fill our lives up with things: jewellery, cars, houses, clothes, and we all seem to want to be famous. We are consumed by our desire to accumulate "things to make us happy". But do any of these material things make us happy, really? No. They're all superficial and have only a fleeting effect and furthermore, they encourage everyone to constantly compete to top what they already have.

South Koreans also have a love of luxury goods; like people anywhere, they don't always live up to their ideals.

The idea of clearing out any superficial clutter from our lives makes sense to me. I've experienced how the simple, uncluttered design of traditional Korean home interiors promotes a sense of serenity and happiness. I've also seen how Korean women tend to wear flat shoes and comfortable clothes, reflecting the fact that their physical wellbeing is a priority.

Another invaluable lesson towards achieving happiness comes from the teamwork and camaraderie between the *haenyeo*, the women divers of Jeju. How they support and nurture each other, their loyalty and devotion to their group, is *jeong* in action. This bond that joins friends, family and the country together is a vital part of Korea's DNA. *Jeong* is how Korea has not just survived but thrived to become one of the most powerful and influential countries on earth.

Even with North Korea and its atomic weapons only 30 miles away, the streets of Seoul feel so much safer than anywhere else I've been. The divisive politics, economic class divides and gun violence that seem to have infiltrated life in America today make for a stressful and unhappy environment. Whereas when I am in Korea, there is no tension in the air, and no fear of imminent attack. During one visit with my friend Gabriella from Milan, we strolled around Changuimun Gate (one of the eight gates of the fortress wall that surrounded the city during the Joseon dynasty). We marvelled at how tranquil the area was, how peaceful. You can walk the streets in Korea at any time of night and feel safe.

I remember the first time I saw women dressed in *hanbok* in the old part of the city holding signs that read "Please be quiet in the streets". This is also *jeong*. Koreans understand safety and consideration for others is a collective effort – "We before me".

I discovered this first-hand one day when I found myself in a neighbourhood of Seoul I had never visited before called Hapjeong-dong. It's an old industrial area, where the factories have been converted into cool modern apartments, shops, bars and restaurants. It was late afternoon and I was with a friend in a shop trying on clothes. We hadn't eaten and suddenly we were very hungry. We asked the young clerk if she could steer us to a local restaurant. She smiled and giggled, then took us by the hand and led us a few blocks away.

I wondered aloud about her leaving her store with the door wide open, but she assured me that everyone left their doors open. Once again, I was reminded how different life in Seoul is, how much less stressful.

Why are Koreans not fearful? Because they have something else that I see as the key to happiness – grit. They have profound stoicism that has seen them through centuries of war and destruction. They may not be able to change the political situation they find themselves in, but they can, and do, choose to respond to it without fear.

Koreans draw on their inheritance of *han*, *heung* and *jeong*, to triumph over any obstacles. We all have our sorrows, pain, disappointments, frustrations and tragedies, and learning to transform them into positives is profoundly important.

But there is also something else that I think speaks to their happiness – and it is this: Korea is mysterious.

There is even mystery when you receive a gift from a Korean friend. The magnificent wrapping, usually fabric topped with a pretty bow, looks like the gift itself. What could be inside such a precious packaging?

We seem to have lost mystery in our own lives, splashing ourselves everywhere on social media. This self-centred way of being doesn't bring happiness; maintaining a sense of mystery does. Keeping parts of ourselves to ourselves is important for happiness and Koreans know this. We can learn this too.

Just when I think I know Korea, I realise I don't. And that is a great part of its allure.

One time I was extremely frustrated by a lack of Western business understanding on the part of my Korean partners. It's common for my Korean colleagues, many of whom do not speak English, to stick together at international publishing events. I lamented to one that I had adapted to all the changes our business presented, and it was frustrating that they hadn't.

"You have to understand we are like a shrimp between two whales," he said.

I asked for an explanation.

"Korea between China and Japan," he continued. "We have been imprisoned, invaded, kidnapped. We have been the poorest country with great starvation. We are the shrimp."

I shook my head in exasperation, yet I began to understand how Koreans see themselves and why they still turn inward; understandably it's a protective measure. Koreans think of themselves very humbly, too humbly, I think, and they can be hesitant to change. Yet we are in the 21st century now, and Korea is no longer the shrimp, but a whale itself.

It's curious that while *hallyu* has conquered the world, in some ways Korea is still catching up to the idea that it is a global force. I was astounded when I visited the Korean Museum of Art to see an exhibition of the famous painter, Lee Jung-seob, who lived and worked in the 1950s. To my dismay, the only audio and catalogues available were in Korean.

That evening, I was invited to Kyung-sook Shin's home for a farewell dinner. I thanked her for suggesting I see the show but complained about the lack of material in English or other language.

"How can Korea expect tourists to visit if they can't accommodate them?" I asked.

Kyung-sook laughed. "Barbara, Barbara… you see, the problem is that the museum didn't think anyone other than Koreans would like the work."

I couldn't believe it, but it also explained why none of the Korean authors I had discovered had ever been published outside of Korea.

. . . .

There is no perfect place on earth. I know that. And of course, Korea has its problems… and negative aspects. But overall, the general way of being seems to be one of Buddhist peacefulness: of showing loving kindness to ourselves and others. This is expressed in every Korean tradition or custom: honour and respect for others is shown by following the social etiquette, which is practised every day by everyone, from children to the elderly.

Every meal in Korea is a shared experience. Eating in moderation and not wasting food is the Korean way, and part of the reason the country has the greatest longevity on earth. Hiking in nature is the national pastime, while hot springs and massages form part of daily life.

From the philosophy of *han*, I learned that through pain and suffering comes persistence and success.

From *heung*, I learned to savour every morning walk with my dog, to understand that joy is found in nature and culture, in art, film, books and theatre, not in amassing possessions.

And from *jeong*, I found giving to others and being part of a family, whether a biological one or a family of friends, creates a sense of purpose and hope. The sense that we are part of a bigger picture; an interconnected universe, which puts our lives in perspective.

I have studied yoga and meditation for years and have heard all kinds of philosophies and read many books about how to achieve happiness and peace of mind. But it wasn't until I stepped onto Korean soil and experienced their way of being that the lessons came alive to me. I hope that you will be inspired to experience some of these simple, natural ways to improve your life too.

As the wise monk said, "We are happy now."

Acknowledgements

Kyung-sook Shin has inspired my journeys in Korea and I thank her for being my Korean sister and partner in travel, adventure and all the best things in life! Kyung-sook always hopes that when a reader finishes one of her books, they will be kinder to all people. Her compassion and goodness have affected me greatly and she always reminds me to take the higher road, and to be a good person, most of all. She always says each book has its destiny and with the help and friendship of Kyung-sook and others, my book has found its destiny.

I am grateful to my Korean co-agent, Joseph Lee, who was so generous about introducing me to everything delicious, delightful and profound that can be found in his country.

Thank you so much, Martine Koelemeijer of Mo Media in Holland, who first asked me for this book and published it so quickly; she was the first one to make my dream come true. Thank you, a million times, Martine.

I am especially grateful and a million thanks to Sharon Krum for her invaluable abilities in reading every draft from cheering on the seed of the idea to the edited final draft.

And to Sue Park, simply a miracle worker! Sharon and Sue assisted me with fact-checking in Korean and gathering original recipes and other Korean information. Thanks so much to all the recipe contributors; you have added a richness and authenticity of voice that make the book sing.

Thank you, Silvia Valmori of Giunti, who published the book in Italy and supported and nurtured me.

Gabriella Ambrosioni, my dear friend and Italian agent, who not only found the best publisher for the book in Italy, but also became my travel partner in Korea and helped me enjoy some of the best times of my life – she is my Italian sister and made all my adventures more hilarious and profound; simply unforgettable.

And last, but not least, my gratitude knows no bounds when it comes to Aurea Carpenter and Rebecca Nicholson of Short Books, who published my novel *J.M. Barrie Ladies Swimming Society* and gave me a publishing home. I can't think of publishing a book without them. Although Aurea and Rebecca have moved on, they have left me in the capable hands of Evie Dunne, whose talent and insights have helped me shape my manuscript into a book I can be proud of. I am so grateful to Evie and Octopus for bringing such a beautiful edition to English readers.

A very special thank you to my real-life sister, Mary Sue Zitwer Millman, who is like the Rock of Gibraltar to me, always.

And most of all I would like to thank my husband Gil, who is so proud of me and always tells me "Just do you". To have his love, support and confidence means everything to me.

Barbara J. Zitwer is an international literary agent and author of the novel, *The J.M. Barrie Ladies' Swimming Society* (2012). As an agent, she specialises in Korean literature and has launched the international careers of some of the most celebrated, prize-winning Korean authors, including: Booker Prize winner, Han Kang, author of *The Vegetarian* and Man Asian Prize winner, Kyung-sook Shin, author of *New York Times* bestseller, *Please Look After Mom*. She lives in New York City with her husband and their two dogs.